# SOUL RADIANCE

## BRING YOUR SOUL RICHES TO LIFE

Susann Taylor Shier

VELVET SPRING PRESS

Velvet Spring Press
Boulder, Colorado
www.VelvetSpringPress.com

ISBN-10 0-9771232-3-5
ISBN-13 978-0-9771232-3-0
Copyright information available upon request.

Cover Design: Manjari Graphics
Photograph on back cover by Jim Barbour
Interior Design: J. L. Saloff
Typography: Bembo

v. 1.0
First Edition, 2008
Printed on acid free paper.

*Let your Soul take you*

        *where you long to be.*

*To my greatest friend: life itself.*

*And to my daughter, Courtney.*

# CONTENTS

## Part Three:
## A Collection of Soul Journeys

## *Part Four:*
## *Tools for Reunion*

# ACKNOWLEDGEMENTS

*"I am a little pencil in the hand of a writing God who is writing a love letter to the world."*

*--Mother Teresa*

This book has been brought forth by a host of friends and colleagues who have been absolute angels to me. With all my heart I am eternally grateful.

I thank the many beautiful Souls who allowed me to share with you their incredible sessions, filled with their profound experiences and the wealth of the Soul journeys they took to reunite with the riches of their Soul gifts. I am deeply appreciative for all of my other clients whose astonishing inner- and outer-life journeys of transformation have been a springboard for the depth of what has been brought forward in this book.

Thank you from the bottom of my heart to the many friends who continually inspire and encourage me, showing up in so many remarkable ways. I am surrounded by so much talent and love.

A very specific thank you to my essential ingredient on all levels, my editor, John Kadlecek. Thank you Amy Bayless, for your dedication. There would be no book without your ability to take my handwritten pages and produce readable, typed pages. My gratitude pours out to Naomi Bauer and Cara Bradley for their skill and care in transcribing the sessions. My hats off to the fine proof reading of Sharon Garrett and excellence of design work by Jamie Saloff. I am in thankful awe to Nance Larson and Peter Kafka for their heartfelt and truthful assistance in the conveyance of "My Soul Journey." Deep thanks to Elvira Colburn, for her thrill in bringing the light of clarity to this valuable material. My admiration for Diana Keck and Karen Frankel and their thoughtful input. Thank you Cindy Pillmore for your wisdom that came at just the right moments. I have such appreciation for Kimberly Bryant and Scarlett Joy for assisting me in a myriad of ways to keep the rest of my life moving around this book. Thank you Aaron Krieshok, for your remarkable skill in producing the CD for the book. And what would I do without my computer wizard, Scott Mesch. And congratulations to Manjari Henderson for another fabulous book cover and to Jim Barbour for his excellent photography.

And to you, the reader, my honor and respect for the path you have taken that has led you to choose to bring forth your Soul's Radiance. May your time and energy with this book reward you in immense ways.

Clients whose stories are included in this book happily gave me permission to use their session. A few even mentioned how satisfying it is for them to know that their work could be helpful to others. This generosity means so much to me.

The sessions have been edited somewhat, so that the reader can easily follow them. Everyone gave me their blessing to make adjustments. Of course, all names have been changed to protect individual identities. I am deeply grateful for the collective expression this compilation of sessions provides for each of you to use as you read them, so you can open to and explore for yourself the wealth of what your Soul wishes to bring to your life.

# Part One:

## To Be In Love With Life Itself

# 1

# The Soul's Journey Is Our Song and Life Is Our Dance

This book is for *you*—the you who has glanced up at the night sky, pitch black and filled with mystery, dusted with stars and moon and magic. When you looked into this vast expanse, your body took a deep breath, a sigh, as if to say, "I know you."

This book is for you, who have walked along a sunlit path out beyond the city, the town or the suburbs as you com-muned with the sensation in the air that nature itself emanated. Your body drank in that life force with a grateful, "Thank you for being here with me."

This book is for you who have watched eternity in the ocean waves, the mirrored stillness of a lake or a puddle of fresh rainwater, and breathed in a deep wellspring of essential life, as if to say, "Yes. In this I can rest. In this feeling of connection, I can know peace."

Maybe you are someone who feels bumped around, like a bumper car, in your outer life, and long with every fiber of your being to be able to leave it all behind. Just for a moment, just for a day, perhaps. You have a sense of the home you came from but you don't know the way there.

There *is* a way to experience what your Soul is longing to know that feels just beyond your reach. You *can* receive the gifts of your Soul and know the joy you are longing to have and hold. These gifts of your Soul abide in your very essence, your Soul-Essence. It is connected to everything, everywhere, and is capable of creating everything you could ever imagine or wish for. It is alive and well deep within you, available to become the full-bodied expression of you. Your Soul's radiance springs from this boundless expanse of all your Soul-Essence is part of. It is the key to opening the door for all your dreams coming into fruition.

Your Soul is connected to all that was you before you were born. Your Soul is infinite and connected to the vastness of the Divine. It is the beloved component of you that is always present, always connected to universal wisdom. Sit back and let your Soul's love for all that you are in this magical human dimension transform you moment by moment and take you where you long to be. You will have abundant means to connect with the treasure of your Soul gifts and the dimensions of your Soul's essence through the pages of this book and the topics of the sessions generously shared here.

Stop for a moment to imagine what you would like your Soul to participate in manifesting of your goals and dreams. Jot them down and take stock of what is valuable to you. Remember, the Soul dwells in the field of limitless possibilities. Nothing is too big or too unimportant from the perspective of the Soul. Nothing is selfish from the Soul's vantage point. As long as the Soul is involved, you don't have to worry if you are just hearing your ego speaking. Your Soul's job is to connect you continually with all that is of the Divine. Allow it to be present for you so that you can manifest the wealth of life experience you choose for yourself.

You may feel that you are great at imagining what you want, but not so great at manifesting it. You feel a significant gap between what you want and what you are able to make real in your life. You certainly are not alone! I have heard this quandary expressed by many in the last few years, especially now that we are collectively beginning to see how it is possible we create our reality, and especially since we have opened ourselves to discover the law of attraction that states (From the *Wikipedia*

*Encyclopedia*): "A person's thoughts (conscious and unconscious), emotions and beliefs cause a change in the physical world that attracts positive or negative experiences that correspond to the aforementioned thoughts, with or without the person taking action to attain such experiences. This process has been described as 'harmonious vibrations of the law of attraction', or 'You get what you think about; your thoughts determine your experience'."

What we put our attention on is what we create. And being able to feel what we wish to manifest is very helpful. These are terrific steps that have been identified by many for years. Many people understand these principles and have diligently applied them, but the manifestation part of the equation remains elusive. The question has widely become: How do I manifest something that is beyond the range of my experience? How do I manifest the money or income I want when I have never known what it feels like to have it? How do I feel something I can't get in touch with like assurance or assertiveness, etc.? How do I attract the love of my life, my Soulmate, and feel what it feels like to have him or her in my life, when I have never known anything remotely close to that?

These questions have been brought to me through the work I have dedicated myself to for 15 years—to help people get in touch with their Soul gifts, strengths and purposes. These questions are what have prompted this book and it will allow you to uncover the answers to these questions for yourself. Let your Soul take you where you long to be. That is why it is there.

*Soul Radiance* is the guide which leads you to experience everything your heart desires. It will assist you to connect with the wealth of your Soul-Essence, your connection to universal wholeness and wisdom, which leads to everything your heart desires.

There are 20 sessions in this book describing the Soul journeys I have taken people on in our sessions together. These journeys take people to the heart of their Soul-Essence to give them the qualities of Spirit they need to bring forth what they are seeking to have in their daily life. This could relate to life purpose, new career possibilities, greater connection with love and intimacy, a more creative connection to their true power source, more money and abundance for living in larger ways, etc. Limitless possibilities are available from the perspective of the Soul when we reunite with its wealth and gifts. The Soul has all we need to fulfill our longings.

You can take your own journey to your Soul-Essence to reunite with the resources of your Soul, connected to all that truly feeds you. The power of these journeys is demonstrated in the pages that follow. A guided meditation is provided at the end of the book.*

As you "journey" to the space of your Soul-Essence you will connect to and experience the qualities of Spirit that are the building blocks that bring you into divine union with what you are longing to manifest. Whether it is a new car, a better relationship or more fun in your life, what you hold divine union with inside you is naturally reflected in your outer world. This is a universal law at work. What you have created from your Soul-Essence with utter assurance and joy will radiate from you as naturally as the rays from the sun pour forth every day. Soul radiance is the gift of your finest self to the world. There you are, in all your brilliance and splendor, in love with life itself.

*A CD of the guided meditation is available to order at
www.SoulMastery.net

# 2

# INTUITION:
# THE VOICE OF THE SOUL

We are all born with natural intuitive abilities. Our intuition is the means for us to hear Spirit speaking through us. When we listen to our intuitive voice, we have the means for living from the voice of our Soul. Listening to and acting on your intuition is a primary ingredient in bringing forth your Soul's radiance and bringing your Soul riches to life.

To begin to develop your intuition, ask life, God, the Divine or the universe what it has to share with you. Let yourself be open to your Soul's gifts and purposes, streaming through your heart. Let yourself tune in to your core that is always present to connect you to your Soul wealth and wisdom. The following description of the certainty of this core place within us, which can always be listened to, says it so clearly. It is from an article entitled "Clinging to the Core," from www.dailyom.com.

"While it is perfectly natural and part of our process to locate our sense of self in externals, anytime those external factors shift, we have an opportunity to rediscover and move closer to our core, which is the only truly safe place to call home. The core of our being is not affected by the shifting winds of circumstance. It is as steady and consistent as the sun. Like the sun, there are times when our core seems to be inaccessible to us, but this is just a misperception. We know that when the sun goes behind a cloud or sets for the night, it has not disappeared but is temporarily out of sight. In the same way, we can trust that our inner core is always shining brightly, even when we cannot quite see it. We can cling to this core, knowing that an inexhaustible light shines from within ourselves; knowing that our home is that bright sun shining in our core."

We must engage our heart to truly hear our intuitive wisdom. When we hear and receive our Soul's wisdom through the heart, it can be trusted. You might be saying, "That all sounds well and good, but I know my heart is cluttered, confused and shutdown. I'm afraid of being hurt. I don't pay much attention to my heart unless I'm crying with sadness."

That is often why people aren't able to get in touch with their intuition or their Soul's voice or their feeling of being connected spiritually. Until Spirit flows through your heart, you may feel expanded and uplifted momentarily, but you don't have your Soul gifts and strengths available to radiantly activate your Soul in your life. This does mean that your heart needs to be tended to, and the barriers moved away to make room for your Soul's joy to shine through.

Paramount in this process of opening and filling the heart with divine connection is tapping into your Soul's resources so they flood in to feed your heart. When the true food is present, the blocks and false protection mechanisms dissolve as they are replaced with that which has much greater value to your heart and Soul. The river is undammed and your Soul riches may come to life. But, if the heart is filled with fear or grief on a continual basis, the river of life cannot flow through it. You only feel fear when you are consciously or unconsciously guarding your heart from perceived harm. This protection does not allow your heart to be filled with the true Soul food that it needs to hold the strength necessary to realize that nothing can harm the heart that is connected to pure Love and divine strength. As you relieve the heart of the constraints creating the protection, the space may be opened to welcome the Soul's riches. As the heart is happy and full, it is in a position to be available to intuitive guidance and its application in our life. Our "spiritual practice" is not for the purpose of feeling high and expanded. We are spiritual beings living through a consciousness experiencing the creation of life in a physical capacity. Allowing our Soul to speak through our heart and all our capacities for expression *is* our spiritual practice.

After filling your heart with a sense of love and appreciation, it is open to receive, and you are ready to take the next step. Listen with your heart as you open to your Soul. Be open to listen to a higher, more expanded dimension.

Like most, I have had to uncover my intuitive voice. As I focus my attention and listen for it in my personal meditative practice, it comes forward. My meditation may be a specifically allotted time for my Soul's voice to speak, or a moment in the midst of the day that I give deliberate space to breathe deeply and acknowledge my connection to the Divine through my heart and Soul. Whatever the outer circumstance, I first put attention on my heart and bring the spirit of appreciation or thankfulness to the moment. I then create an openness to receive and give expression to the voice of my Soul that is always available to guide my life's movements. This voice comes as an intuitive message, either through words, images, sensations, or a combination. It's different each time for me.

It takes time and practice to know the difference between your intuitive voice and those sabotaging voices of doubt, fear and mistrust in your head. I love sharing tools that teach you how to know the difference in a very practical application. Once you have learned to discern the difference and practice from your intuitive voice, you are ready to take the next step. Trust your intuitive voice, whether it comes through sound, sight, feeling or a sense of knowing or a symbolic message. It is vital to declare that you are going to follow your Soul, no matter what. It is essential to create that place in yourself that knows your Soul can be trustworthy.

Learn to trust this friend who may feel brand new, but has always been with you. Remember, it is your Soul speaking, and that is what you truly wish to have guide your life. Let your Soul take you where you long to be. As you develop a relationship with it through listening, trusting and practicing the art of letting it guide you, the bond is forged and you merge with its wisdom and loving support. The intuitive voice of your Soul becomes a treasured friend and mentor living within you. This allows your Soul's infinite gifts and wisdom to come into your life.

Living from your Soul's voice is not only the greatest gift you can give yourself, it is also the greatest resource you can give your children. Children listen to and watch for who you are much more than what you say. If you are following your Soul's guidance, you will find yourself happy, easygoing, confident and clear. This is the divine mentoring a child longs for from their "Godparent," their "parent of God." True parenting is teaching children to trust their inner guidance and live from that truth. As you hold and value this space of connection, you pave the way for your children to do the same. And your children are not just your physical children. They are aspects of your inner world, all those in your world who play with you in the journey of life. As you trust your guidance system, your Soul's GPS, you learn to trust others in your life. You are trustworthy as a friend and partner.

To ignite your intuition, the first step is listening. The second step is acting on the voice you hear, no matter how new, small or simple it sounds, especially in comparison to the mind chatter you are accustomed to hearing. Remember, your Soul is connected to all knowledge and all wisdom and Divine Love. Your intuition allows you access to that expansive, truth-oriented field of resources, always available.

I encourage you to trust it. Have the courage to stand up for your heart's desire, and be true to your spiritual values by listening to the intuitive voice that gives your spirit expression. To live from your Soul's radiance requires not just contemplating living a spiritual path, but passionately acting on your Soul's voice so you can move in the ways you long to and do what you know is yours to do.

# 3

# FULFILLING
# YOUR SOUL'S LONGINGS

Is your desire in life really your Soul calling for its fulfillment? What if the longings you feel are your Soul's way of reconnecting you to the wealth of your Soul-Essence and the universal abundance it is connected to? The specific experiences that we wish to create in our lives to make us happy, free or fulfilled come from our Soul nudging us to know the fulfillment that we sense deep inside is real for us.

But how do you know what fulfills you? How do you know which desires really give you the deep, Soulful satisfaction you wish for? How do you get your Soul purpose to be more than a vague sense, existing just beyond your conscious grasp?

I invite you to experience the incredible wealth your Soul has to give to your life. It always has the accurate, abundant, love-filled component for your life fulfillment the moment you are open to receive it. Ask, and it certainly will be given. No matter what the concerns, the heartaches, the confusion and the seemingly unsolvable situations, each time you call on the Soul for "the answer," it will deliver.

You may wonder, "How can some element of me, called my Soul, know what I need right now? How can this invisible source I'm not in touch with understand me? How can I connect with a spiritual dimension to resolve, or even have a bit of insight about, my situation?"

Through the magic of Spirit at work, your creative Soul plays its natural guiding role for your life. Inherent in your Soul is the wisdom to know what is required for your Soul's purpose and fulfillment. The reunion of the physical *you* with the Soul-Essence produces your Soul's radiance shining through your capacities. Your Soul-Essence, which resides in the very core of your Soul and has an influence on the life force of every cell within you, is connected to All That Is. It is bathed in peace and pure Love. It is continually fed by the power of connection to Source. It is whole. Oneness resounds through it. Your Soul-Essence is connected to all universal wisdom and Divine Love where every possibility for creation lives.

Your Soul springs from that Soul-Essence, which is connected to all of creation. Your Soul is made up of the riches of your Soul gifts, strengths and purposes that you brought with you. Your Soul carries the uniqueness of elements that makes you who you are through the radiance of its expression in your life.

Our longings and desires are the way the Soul works through us to help us get reconnected to those places we have missed and with which we are now choosing to reengage. Our Soul song wants to be sung more fully through every aspect of our existence. How would you have longed for a relationship, more money or an exciting career if you didn't know, somewhere inside you, that it was a real possibility for you? Just as we can't physically give voice to a sound or a word we haven't heard, so we can't experience something we haven't "heard" first in our Soul.

Everything you need you *have* known at a Soul level. What you need to do now is simply reconnect and reunite with your Soul-Essence in that area in your body or feeling realm where you feel a particular lack. Your feeling of lack springs from a place in you that has not been listening to your Soul's voice, whispering to you about how to create what makes your heart sing. The key to manifestation lies within you as you are reunited with the wealth of your Soul-Essence. That Soul-Essence is connected to all of Divinity. It can take care of all of your needs and desires.

Put your attention on the qualities of Spirit you wish to have. As spiritual resources fill your cells, feel renewed and more alive than ever. Thus, problems, pain, or lack fall away. These lacks within you are merely the places you have held separate from your Soul and Spirit. These are the places feeling the pain. The lack of life force as hurt, anger, abandonment, fear, etc., has held the space where Spirit used to feed your life force. Your choices have led you to the pain of separation. It shows up as emotional distress, mental confusion, physical pain or even spiritual emptiness. As you bring in the resource of connection to Spirit that is relevant to the need at hand, the pattern of separation dissolves. You are replacing the old pattern with the quality of Spirit that you now value more.

Where did these patterns come from that I am referring to which create the pain of separation we experience? And how do we release these blocks that prevent us from being naturally connected to our Soul gifts? I call these patterns or blocks barnacles on the Soul. They come with us into our incarnations as imprints or adjuncts to our inherent Soul strengths and purposes. They translate as or become self-sabotaging mechanisms that plague us in our daily life. This can manifest as relationship challenges, such as continually picking inappropriate love interests. It can be reflected in the inability to step up to create a career choice that makes us feel good about getting up in the morning. These imprints can keep us from being able to fuel our life with the monetary resources we sense we are capable of producing.

The sessions in Part Three give ample scenarios of what these barnacles can look like in our every day life situations. It is valuable to identify these barnacles that reveal themselves as the lacks or limitations we feel. They dissolve when we reunite with the riches of the Soul that re-establish the avenues for personal fulfillment we are seeking in place of the old patterns that no longer serve us.

These barnacles also keep us from knowing the ecstatic pleasure of living in this abundantly alive world. One client creatively described this occurrence in the following words when he expressed the dilemma of limitation he was working with. "I buried the treasure of my Soul and all the resources, and I can't find them. I under packed for the voyage here."

We come to Earth as Souls who have had previous experience beyond this world. We developed our Soul strengths and purposes that we might bring them as part of our gifts to humanity, along with our desire to experience the abundance of life this amazing Earth has to offer.

In numerous sessions, my clients and I have uncovered the fact that Souls coming here have left various resources at the border of the Earth plane for a number of reasons.

The following is a brief description of some of the ways we as a general population have created limitations held at the deep, subterranean level, keeping us from recognizing our Soul's radiance and our ability to operate from the divine space of limitless possibilities.

a) Many have left a portion of their gifts and strengths behind because their first glance at the beings living here have made them feel as though there was no place for the brightness and strength of what they were bringing. Consequently, they took on the attitude, "When in Rome, do as the Romans do." They thought they would be better off to turn down the dimmer switch on their brightness and true power so they could be like everyone here. There is a strong magnetic pull in human beings to belong.

Our Soul knows oneness with every aspect of life, and then we arrive in a world filled with people who live in separation from their Spirit and this oneness. There is an instinct to try to change that pattern and bring everyone out of separation and into oneness. That is natural. And this desire can also bring with it the human need to belong to whatever is most dominant. "Majority rules" is the name of the game. The human need to belong distracts Souls coming here and makes them forget the spiritual connection that shows we are already one in essence:

Soul to Soul. When Souls come here with their bright selves and it is not so bright here, the feelings of isolation, loneliness and alienation can take over. Again, there seems to be a choice made to forget the Soul's heritage, which knows universal oneness of connection with each Soul.

When the truth of oneness is held in the heart, isolation, loneliness and alienation dissolve. Awareness of being one with the true majority is held. Just think about it. On a universal scale everything is connected and supports your brilliance. There is just a thin band of human consciousness here that is out of alignment with that picture. Where does majority rule in truth? The majority we already belong to is the universal consciousness of oneness. Staying aligned with one's Soul-Essence, which is connected to all that is life, allows us to be part of the true majority. When we have opted to align with the human consciousness mired in separation through our need to belong to whatever appears to be dominant, then we are opting, by free choice, to let go of the connection, support, love, strength and communion with what truly feeds our Soul and heart and life blood. In each moment we are choosing to be connected to the riches of our Soul-Essence or to buy into the group consciousness of separation that exists here. When we opt to "belong to" or be part of this level of separation from universal oneness, we, by default, leave our Soul treasures behind.

b) We could also have deliberately left our gifts, such as our brightness, behind because they were sacred to us and we sensed the Earth might not have appreciated all that we were made of. So, at a Soul level, we might have left our magnificence at the border to be able to blend in with the dull consciousness present here. It can be a very practical decision, but at a Soul level it doesn't serve us. For instance, if we go on a camping trip, it would seem practical to leave our musical instruments at home, but at a Soul level it could be a magical enhancement to all involved to bring some instruments as a means of sharing our heart and Soul on the trip.

c) Some who have come here dedicated to be of service have found themselves betraying their connection to what is sacred and true and of integrity within their heart and Soul to forget themselves to help others. They often find themselves losing connection to their brightness of Divinity because they "come down" to try to lift others up. Consequently, they get caught in the trap of putting others first at a core level and their gifts slowly diminish. They run out of their Soul resources and end up with nothing inside or nothing to give, and wonder what has gone awry in their lives.

d) Another scenario I have witnessed frequently in clients occurs during their Soul's journey in coming to Earth. A Soul can be guided by information that does not serve their purposes. We have all had a time in our life when we followed the direction or instruction of someone, whether it be a relative, friend or stranger, and discovered it was not working for our best interest. We chose to follow their direction rather than our internal knowing of what was most valuable at a Soul level for ourselves. In that moment, maybe listening to someone else provided a sense of feeling wanted or potential connection, but it did not fill us with true Soul food, just someone else's idea of what might be good for us. This can happen at a Soul level, also. During a client's Soul journey, I have seen many incidents that conveyed a time when the client listened to the voice of another Soul, guiding them in the ways of the world that were not aligned with their heart's direction. This could happen before a Soul even gets here to the Earth.

When we allow ourselves to be misled, this guidance may include instructing us to leave our gifts and brightness behind, as if to say they aren't needed here or welcome here. The Soul that is newer to the Earth scene can be very thankful to have a mentor or guide. They forget to check in with their heart to see if this mentor is speaking from their own heart and Soul. This situation is parallel to a common situation that we have all found ourselves in: listening to our heads, not our heart or gut. We are guided by "should" or "this will help me feel accepted," etc.

Fortunately, the Soul is very malleable and open to change. Thank goodness. Reconnecting to the buried treasure of Soul resources left behind is quite simple. Having guided people in this reconnective journey, I can testify to that. It is as simple as closing the car trunk with your suitcase in it, remembering that you forgot to pack your toothbrush, and running upstairs to get it. You tuck it in your purse or traveling bag and off you go with the satisfaction that you now are complete and have all you need for a great trip. It works the same at a Soul level. When we realize we are missing something in our life we can simply reunite with the wellspring of our Soul-Essence to resource what we believe is missing. Reunion with our Soul-Essence is the natural way to bring forth our Soul's radiance and have the life we desire.

What we hold in our hearts and what we hold in consciousness manifests. We become an expression of the very essence or quality that we hold as most valuable in any moment. Let it be your Soul gifts radiantly moving through your heart and mind that ignites what you manifest.

Put your attention on what you are valuing most in this very moment. For example, imagine that what you value most in this moment is the craving you have for chocolate. Isn't the craving really for a quality of experience? Is it peace, comfort, pleasure, energy, vitality or love? Aren't these qualities of Spirit?

If you love watching sports events, your Soul wants you to know more of certain qualities, like direction, teamwork or success. Watching sports can give you those feeling experiences vicariously. It's good to notice what longing the sport of your choice portrays. Then it's even better to let those qualities be active in you so you can feel them all the time.

If you want to attract a new relationship, you might have made a long list of what you want in that man or woman. Details are essential, but when you truly focus your heart on what matters most to you, you will discover that it is qualities of Spirit in that person you most deeply want to draw to you.

If you have a certain need from a relationship, it is a quality of Spirit you are longing to know that you believe this relationship will give you. You want the partner you are with to be around more. The truth is, you might need more comfort, nurturing or reassurance that you are lovable. Or you want your partner to get off the couch and go get a job, or do something productive. You want a more assertive, directed, powerful energy in your life.

Take a moment to go deeper in your heart and ask yourself what experience you really long for. Then deeper still, what quality of Spirit do you really want to know in this moment? Yes, you want it to come from your partner, but if you could reach to your Soul to have it, you would have instant gratification and no one to blame for not providing the experience you feel you are lacking. So much freedom and power is available this way!

A year ago I went to a performance of aerial dancers called "Frequent Flyers." I was compelled to take a class in aerial dance/low-flying trapeze, and have continued with the classes ever since. Just before I started the classes I realized that I had been longing to find a greater sense of freedom within me. As I discovered what that first class freed up in me, I realized that my Soul compelled me to take these classes to bring a greater sense of freedom, fearlessness and joy to all of me, especially my body. Knowing this, I could not only look forward to the classes, but also live an "aerial-dancer" Spirit more in my life.

Longings and desires activate movement, expansion and creation. As you become more aware that it is a quality of experience, a quality of Spirit, you are reaching for, your choices in life can take on a whole new meaning. You are not asking the outer world to fulfill you. You are allowing the riches of your Soul-Essence to meet your heart's desires. Let your Soul take you where you long to be. Let your outer world reflect the qualities of Spirit you have reunited with. Abundance at a Soul level streaming into your lifeblood, allows you to manifest the pleasures of life you choose to align with (the chocolate, the sports event, the relationships, etc.) that reflect the abundance you are radiating within you. The chocolate digests, the sports event is over, the relationship changes continually. The gifts of your Soul are a part of you for life.

The sensations of the body and the longings in the emotional realm are real signals for us to listen to. They work together to signal the voice of the Soul speaking through us. Dr. Christiane Northrup says that there is an immensely powerful connection between the physical and emotional realms of life. There are literally hundreds of studies demonstrating how separation or lack of support from family can negatively affect the immune system and contribute to autoimmune disease. Similarly, studies suggest that an inability to harness emotions such as hostility can cause heart attacks, and medical studies on breast cancer link feelings of powerlessness in relationships to a lessened probability of beating the cancer.

We are not just angels playing harps and holding spiritual connection. We get to explore and give radiant expression to the facets of Spirit's jewels of joy, peace, ecstasy, freedom and power, to name a few. Our body and emotions signal to us where we are experiencing limitation or blocks to life force igniting our life movement. These signals come to our awareness because we have proclaimed our longing for more creative, expanded, meaningful experiences. The emotional or physical signals are the old patterns we are ready to replace with more Soulful ingredients: Divine Love where fear has been, courage where doubt has been. The Soul is asking us to connect to the qualities of Spirit we are longing for. We must go beyond trying to solve the emotional or physical situations. As we listen to the voice of our Soul we learn to give ourselves what we truly wish to manifest.

Negative emotions connect us to the places in our body where we are disconnected from our Soul's wealth. We feel pain or discomfort in some part of our body to let us know where there is a need for a greater quality of Spirit that our Soul is longing to connect us with.

For instance, if anger appears, or if we are feeling a restriction physically that creates a response of anger in us, it has appeared in a place in ourselves where our inherent divine power, born of absolute connection to Spirit and our Soul's strength, is not being held, known or given expression. We are angry that we are not connected to our power. A feeling of helplessness may also tie in here. We feel helpless when we feel powerless, as though it is not possible to reconnect to our true power source.

If we are feeling sad, this experience carries in its core a longing for connection to the Divine, and most often to Divine Love. The grief is our heart, crying out to reconnect with love in the place where our loss of connection to Divine Love has been held or known.

Fear can show up in a myriad of experiences as a reminder that we are not holding absolute knowing that our connection, through our heart and Soul to the All That Is, is in operation for us continually. Fear shows up in all the places and all the moments that we imagine we are limited in some way. We fear we aren't in command of our life or we won't be able to return to that place of being in command. Truly being in command stems from feeling absolutely connected to Spirit while absolutely trusting its guidance in co-creation with us. This can only be true if we are open in our heart and Soul to let universal wisdom and power and love command our life. Only then do we have what it takes to bring forth the magic of life that flows like a stream of ease and generosity abundantly moving in our life.

These emotional experiences are present as gateways to allow us to open to the true qualities of Spirit we are longing to have pulsating in our very bloodstream. Let these emotional experiences, which represent parts of yourself cut off from Spirit, be recognized and connected to the divine essence they are crying out for. Acknowledging the anger, sadness and fear you feel is a vital dimension of bringing forward your Soul radiance in all the aspects of your life.

Our longings come from our Soul, and our desire to manifest stems from our Soul's desire to be given fruitful magnification in our life. In this realm of creation called manifestation, the power of intention is an essential starting point. As you take this first step of stating what it is you truly want, you are remembering that you are a truly powerful creator. Intention directs the attention of your longing.

Step two comes through bringing your focus of attention to *feeling* what it is you long for. Feeling awakens the participation of your cells and gives creative juice to your desire and intention.

But what part does the Soul play? What knowledge and wisdom does the Soul wish to share that is essential for the revelation and fruition of all that our hearts long to bring forth of our Soul riches? We, as Souls, are connected to a universal energy field that says anything is possible. It is the field of limitless possibilities. And the universe continually says, "Your wish is my command."

Your Soul loves to take you where you long to be. So, knowing that your Soul, through its connection to your Soul-Essence, has everything you could ever imagine within its reach, isn't it wise, practical and wonderful to be in touch with your Soul riches? And since your Soul dwells within you and is present to allow the universal wholeness to come into your living reality, doesn't it make sense to want to get in touch with these Soul riches, so your life can flourish from the place of connectedness, abundance and joy?

I spoke to a woman recently who said she was completely overwhelmed with family issues. She said she wanted to have a session to make a greater connection to her Soul and Source, hoping she might find a solution, or just get out of her misery for a moment. But she couldn't do the session. She couldn't move on what her inner guidance wanted for her, because she had this family issue to deal with first. She said once she got that settled, and once she felt support from them again, maybe then she would have the time, energy and finances to do what she was longing to do, which included connecting to her Soul-Essence and its wisdom, and connecting to universal intelligence.

I gently reminded her that she couldn't solve the problem at the level of the problem. The problem for her at that moment was the lack of understanding and camaraderie she was feeling within herself. Where to get those resources she longed for? In this case she was hoping her family would supply them and was dismayed that they were not.

Her Soul and all that it is connected to is fully capable, available and willing to gift her with these resources as soon as she "downloads" them from their Source. She doesn't need to fight and stress for something that isn't available right now, in the way she imagines she wants it, from family members who aren't in the position to supply it. When you are depleted in an area, you can't attract that quality to you at the physical level. She needed to open to receive the quality from a Soul level, where it already exists. She understood that.

To manifest something in life, whether it is a car, an intimate relationship, or a career that you love pouring yourself into, it is essential to get in touch with, first and foremost, the quality of Spirit that you wish to manifest. Everything starts as energy. You must ask yourself, "What is the nature of the energy I actually want to create? What is the quality of Spirit that I actually wish to manifest when I say I want a car or an intimate relationship?" It is unique for each one of us. One person wants a car for a greater sense of freedom, another wants a car for a greater sense of power, and another wishes to know the security a car gives.

The vital element in manifesting our dream is our ability to name and get in touch with the quality of Spirit or experience we want. What is the quality of Spirit money represents to us that we actually want, when we say we want more money? When we ask ourselves this vital question, we can begin to manifest from the level of our Soul. These qualities of Spirit we are truly going for can come from a place of universal abundance, through our Soul, into our heart and life. This is what it means to bring our Soul riches to life, to allow our Soul gifts to be brought into living experience. We say we want money, a better career, a more fulfilling relationship, and our next step is to get in touch with the Soulful qualities we truly long for. Then, all of creation conspires to bring us the wealth that has value to us. When our choices are aligned with our Soul and its power, creation is effortless. We can feel our Soul purpose being fulfilled because we create and manifest from the level of our Soul.

Yes, it is vital to know how it feels to have the car, or to be in an intimate relationship, or to be successful in the career of choice in order to manifest any one of them. This is the point where many get stuck. It does not seem to be enough for us to try to feel what it feels like to have something. There appears to be a gap between what we think or feel, and putting our intention on manifesting, and our ability to have that thought or feeling produce results. For many there is a lack of deep-seated *knowing* that what we long for can actually be created. Our thoughts and feelings are aligned, but at the core of our being our heart and Soul have not been brought into the equation. This key element of having our life force be a hundred percent engaged is not present. And that's the missing link. Our Spirit must be ignited for any real degree of creation to happen. It seems like a paradox, how to feel one with something you have never experienced.

"How do I manifest an intimate, deeply loving relationship if nothing in me has ever experienced that? How do I act as though it is already present when it is completely foreign to me? How do I attract the cash flow I want when I grew up surrounded by beliefs of poverty and lack, which I took in like a sponge? How do I feel I already have that money and sense abundance? I don't have a clue."

The Soul DNA holds the memory of what it feels like to have that quality of experience we dream of. That is how we are able to dream and create something outside of the context of what we have known in our life thus far. We tap into it. Maybe it is unknown at the conscious level, but there is a sense of knowing at a Soul level that what we long for and strive for is possible! Our Soul knows how to bring to us the qualities of Spirit that we need to allow our outer world to reflect those qualities.

For instance, if we want to expand an aspect of our world, we must first expand the field of inner qualities or resources that would give birth to that outer expansion. "As above, so below." Visually, this has the look of an hourglass. The "heaven" of what we wish to create and expand comes first and moves through us to be brought to fruition in the physical plane. If we want a new career, we must generate the qualities, the "heaven" of what that career carries for us. If we want a new relationship or a greater sense of intimacy in our existing relationship, we must connect with and live from that new place within ourselves first. Our Soul allows us to touch into the resources and qualities of Spirit that will allow us to create in new ways. Our Soul allows us to get in touch with a sense of knowing that the new endeavor or the new approach to a relationship is joyfully doable. Each of the journey sessions in Part Three give an example of how our expansion to greater qualities of Spirit, through connecting with our Soul-Essence, allows us to achieve the life direction we are longing for. This sense of assurance is the foundation for manifesting from a Soul level.

There is nothing that the Soul cannot tackle. Everything we see as an issue or problem is a creative challenge that the Soul has the "solution" for. Remember, the Soul is connected to all that exists in the field of universal creation. Soul-filled resolution can apply to any pattern that we may feel a victim of, where we feel no way out. A therapist said to me, "Once a person had abandonment issues those issues will follow them through life." I don't agree. I have witnessed many clients heal that wound and other wounds of the same intensity by contacting the aspect of their Soul-Essence that they abandoned along the way. Our abandonment of our Soul gifts in a moment of innocent misunderstanding causes the ensuing pattern of attracting abandonment scenarios in our life. When we reunite with our Soul's wholeness abandonment no longer plagues us. The universe opens its loving doors of connection to us.

This assurance is in complete contrast to the fear of the unknown that permeates our existence quite frequently. As a human race, we seem to prefer living with the known that we are in the midst of, regardless of how painful the situation is, rather than open to the unknown that lies before us. We imagine that the unknown is bound to be worse—an odd quirk in the collective psyche, for sure. We don't allow ourselves to be open to the magic of life that the unknown potential has waiting for us once we "let go of the side of the pool", and immerse ourselves in the deep, clear, limitless waters of magical possibility.

Lying at the root of this fear of the unknown is our propensity to let go of the connection to the Divine when we move into new territory. We seem to think that if we are moving into something new, whether an outer skill or an inner way of viewing our lives, we should rely on the mind to guide us to this new place. It appears to be an old habit or protection mechanism to check with the mind first to see how it would handle the new situation. The mind, in and of itself, is often present to protect us, so the mind and fear naturally go together when it is not being ignited by the heart and Soul. Hence, we find ourselves fearful of what the mind cannot grasp by itself.

As we embark on the ever-changing journey of life and are mindful to stay in our conscious, heart-centered connection to Spirit, our Soul guides us and takes care of us, very thoroughly, every step of the way. To know Spirit holds us is a truth of existence that we can absolutely count on, allowing us to move into the unknown, which is never an unknown in the hands of Spirit. Our connection to Spirit is our anchor of knowing, no matter what changes happen in our unfolding spiritual adventure called life.

The following is an example of how we always have exactly the guiding Light we need within our Soul to move into any "unknown" that comes into our scope of experience.

I had a client, Sheila, come to me, weeping and feeling terrified because her boyfriend had stopped seeing her. She couldn't imagine that he was out of her life, nor could she imagine what she would do without him. He was such a loving, kind and caring Soul for her, and she felt empty and shattered and her heart ached physically. The panicky feelings that accompanied the heartache brought her to me in tears of hopelessness.

We took a journey to her Soul-Essence. We both knew that somewhere deep inside her was a connection to a place that could anchor a knowing that she would be taken care of. We had to walk gently through her forest of disbelief that anyone cared, or that she had the faith to believe that anyone could care. The deepest part of the forest was the place of disbelief that there even *was* a divine source of caring for her in this huge universe. This was her core place of separation. She had a horrific feeling of isolation that gripped her like a vice, saying, "Nothing in heaven or Earth cares about me or even knows I exist." Just as she was about to step into that seeming abyss of emptiness, the space of her Soul's knowing and pure Love shone brightly before her. She stepped into a space she instantly called "mama love." It was the space of pure Love that wrapped around every cell in her body, around her whole being, and extended around her entire self like a huge embrace of warm, soft, gentle, reassuring care. "All is well. I am always here. You can rest eternally in me," were the words emanating from this loving embrace. Sheila's blissful smile flowed from every part of her, inside and out. She was home in the arms of pure Love.

She could let this man go, a man who really didn't get her, she said honestly. And she could now rest in, and feel the deep sense of merging with, that "mama love" that she was really looking for and which could now feed her, like a divine umbilical cord.

She was free to attract a man who could truly reflect the space she now held, solidly and lovingly, within her.

We do not need to be in the midst of critical situations to summon our Soul gifts to create from a larger, more plentiful perspective. Everyday situations are just as potent a vehicle for our Soul's deliverance.

A few nights ago I was happily writing. It was a Friday night and I had deliberately said no to an opportunity to go out and play. I knew there was something burning to be written, and this was my time to listen to that inner impulse. And I was having a creative, inspiring time. When I completed the thought, a wave of feeling lonely came over me. Then a few thoughts accompanied it, like, "Why aren't you out having fun? Why are you such a slave to your mission?" I felt another wave of loneliness as I almost bought into the poor-me scenario that was trying to raise its twisted head. It was time to consult with my Soul and leap into that perspective I trusted before the "big, bad wolf" of loneliness tried to ruin the writing party I had just engaged in.

So I took a journey to my Soul-Essence, which I describe in greater detail in the chapter called "Taking a Soul Journey." For me, it has become almost second nature, which I trust can also happen for you. My current favorite Soul song came soaring into my heart. *I live in the heart of God.* I merged with that phrase and brought Light around it as I breathed it more deeply into my heart. I allowed it to flood my heart, and my heartbeat took it to every corner of my body. I felt radiant and full of Divine Love and connection within a few moments. Where was that wave of loneliness? Where was the big, bad wolf? Gone. Not even hanging around in the distance. My party was in full swing again, and I loved every part of it. I was in love with life itself and the joy of creating.

For me, it certainly beats the other options for dealing with the feeling of loneliness. I could have cried myself to sleep in self-pity. I could have rushed out to look for someone or some activity to connect with for a bit of instant but unsatisfying gratification. There are endless possibilities we have managed to come up with to try to temporarily fill the void of loneliness.

When we let our Soul riches come in to replenish the place in ourselves that was separate from Divine Love and connection, we experience a quality of Spirit that never goes away. It is available for our heart and consciousness any time. As we deliberately bring that resource in, it becomes a permanent part of us. We truly expand in our capacity to know genuine fulfillment directly in our life.

It is never selfish to tend our magnificent Soul. Our life depends on it. Our quality of life is a direct manifestation of the degree we tend our Soul. We truly manifest what we are unified with. If our heart is filled with fear, that is what we create. If our heart is filled with Divine Love, that is what we create. We manifest what we are in *divine union* with. We go where our Soul, our Spirit, goes. As our Soul is fully engaged with every aspect of our experience, as we allow our Soul to ignite our life, then we may truly know what it is to embody the riches of joy, peace, confidence, power, freedom and ecstatic pleasure that is our birthright.

Our Soul is wise beyond measure. Our willingness to expand the ways we allow that wisdom into our lives makes all the difference in how we are able to be in our lives. We can survive, manage and cope with the circumstances that keep coming at us, or we can expand our perspective and sense of self to take ourselves freely and joyfully where we long to be. It is a moment-by-moment choice. Our Soul awaits our call.

# 4

# MY SOUL'S JOURNEY

I believe that all of us have had moments, whether they began at age three or just one year ago, when we can remember the radiance of our Spirit peeking through, or maybe leaping forward, in our life. Sometimes it takes a bit of conscious coaxing to recall these magical emergences of Spirit's expansion in us. Some clients have described to me that when they were very young they felt naturally and easily connected to their Soul's voice. They may not have called it that at the time, but as they look back from a more conscious perspective they could describe it this way, with a sense of satisfied recognition that their Soul really was shining through the lattice of their life. Often, due to the ingredients of home, family and the school system, the bringing forth of those inner callings of Spirit were gently pushed into the corner of our inner garden. These callings came back later, when our garden was more ready to flower, or when life circumstances pushed us to reclaim them. At the same time, many have said to me that they never had an inkling of any kind of Soul-level influence bubbling within them for most of their lives.

When I took a closer look at my life before high school, I discovered snippets of Soul whisperings that I did indeed listen to and that kept me going, like placing breadcrumbs on my path so I would be sure not to lose my way in the mirage of shut-down mechanisms I had created for myself when I finally felt safe to come out and play a Soul's game. It's always surprising to see what magic was coming through, even in simple terms, that declared the Soul's guidance was alive and well.

As I walked through life my Soul began to guide me to be interested in spiritual matters. I responded to this voice and acted on it. To listen and say "yes" to the voice of my Soul increasingly took me from being a lost little girl, looking for someone to play God for me, to being the woman I am now, who is in love with life and is vibrantly available to share my wisdom of what it is like to embody the Soul's radiance. My life has been a Soul journey in the simplest and the most profound ways. This has included huge mountains to climb and challenges to be met as my Soul guided me to live in the place of fearless connection to Divine Love. I had to strip away the "barnacles on my Soul," which comprised the patterns of separation I had acquired on life's journey. I was not exempt from a Soul path destined to do some major inner clean-up work. Profound inner work seems to be required from time to time to polish the Soul's radiance to become more clearly in touch with the expansion and fulfillment our Souls long to claim.

My parents divorced when I was 20. They were very considerate to hold off this major life change until my twin sister and I, who were the youngest of four children, had left for college. Their divorce propelled me to begin my search, unconsciously at that point, to start to ask what this thing called love, which I had not witnessed in my childhood, was all about. Embarking on this search meant that I would have to walk through some dark caverns in myself 20 years later, as I unpacked the layers of armor accumulated to keep myself from feeling unloved and unwanted.

When I was 21, my twin sister told me, in passing, that our mother tried to abort us when we were *in utero*. In those days medical abortion was not highly respected in her circles so she secretly drank cod liver oil, which was a popular alternative method, obviously to no avail. My mother felt pressured to terminate the pregnancy because my father told her if she had any more children he would leave. My brother was then 14 months old, and later identified as developmentally disabled, and my other sister was 2 when we were conceived. At the time, this information did not mean much to me. I know now that this challenging way that my life began was a point of Soul choice for me at the deepest level. It was my moment to choose life or death. It was a moment that propelled me, even while still *in utero*, to make the absolute choice to live.

My strong spirit and will to live got me into this world, but I was left with an empty heart that felt unloved and unwanted. As a child, I was quiet, shy and somewhat numb emotionally. That was my way to cope with the fact that I felt disconnected from my family of origin at a Soul level. Deep inside I did not feel they were there for me, nor did they truly understand me. I carried a place in my heart that said I could not be supported in this world, and it was up to me alone to make my life happen.

At age 22 I went to live at Sunrise Ranch, a nonsectarian spiritual community, international headquarters of the Emissaries of Divine Light. I had just graduated from the University of Colorado in Boulder in 1973. Like many my age, I was looking for a brand new approach to life. I was happy to find those who were more than willing to guide me in ways that rang true for me. For me, this was an outward launch into my spiritual journey. I know now that I have always needed a sense of mission and purpose, and this move activated that calling. My Soul's knowing that we are meant to have a place of spiritual family here on earth also propelled me into this community setting. That meant not only would I feel that I was wanted and understood, but others would be on the same page as me and therefore support my Soul's calling to belong to a mission with spiritual values.

The Emissaries of Divine Light had a strong mission to be a unified body radiating "love made visible" into the whole world. Community settings were established around the globe. This community was international in scope. Touching into the sense of the one-world family made my heart sing. I began to awaken to the feeling of being connected to something very grand. Something in me felt supported and I began to deeply relax. I started to wake up and feel safe to express my authentic, outgoing, people-loving self in a much greater way than I ever had before.

After I moved to Sunrise, Peter Kafka created a play based on the book *Jonathan Livingston Seagull* by Richard Bach, and gave me the lead role of Jonathan Livingston Seagull. This opportunity helped me feel seen for the free nature of my heart's expression. I was claiming and expressing my Soul's radiance for the world to see.

In 1974, shortly after I had moved to Sunrise, I was invited to help with the building of a new Emissary center in South Africa. I was thrilled. The magic of spirit opened yet another door for me to go to Capetown and help a leader in the Emissary Program create an Emissary gathering place there. All this was to bring Afrikaners, black Africans and whites together to share in making the One Spirit visible as we worked together and shared gatherings and meals as a diverse, multiracial group.

My mom and dad came to see me at the Sunrise community. They were reassured by our normal country lifestyle. I vividly remember my dad saying to me while we were walking to the large elliptical dome structure that we had built for our service gatherings, "I'm not sure what this is all about but you seem happy, and you have really come out of your shell." It felt great to be validated by my father for something that was so true to my inner purpose, even though it was obviously the unanticipated step I would take after a solid college education.

I was living on a 150-acre property set in the foothills of Loveland, Colorado, with a five-acre organic garden, goats, cows, turkeys, organically grown fields of hay and wheat. I was making butter, yogurt, bread and meals for a hundred people. We valued work as love made visible.

After four years of living with the Sunrise extended family of over one hundred, I met my husband. We came together, based on our love for the purpose of the Emissaries and our mutual love for community and the healing work we both offered there. We married in 1979. It was a magical time for me of coming together on the basis of shared vision and life movement. Seven years later, in 1986, we gave birth to our daughter Courtney. We were birthing a true creative light in human form. Her birth was easy and powerful and utterly breathtaking. To this day I cherish the precious time of first holding her, then beholding her over and over again as she graced our lives. My Soulful relationship with her has been foundational in opening my Soul journey to assist in creating a reunion with the Soul-Essence for so many.

My years of life in a spiritual community hold a truckload of extraordinary and endearing stories too numerous to mention. It was the best of an extended family experience. We worked, played, laughed and devoted ourselves to Spirit together. It was a remarkable setting to raise a child in. My daughter had built-in brothers and sisters of all ages to play with continually. She remembers her first eight years of life at Sunrise Ranch with stars in her eyes. There were abundant gatherings, celebrations and visitors. Each summer we all participated in early morning weeding and harvesting in the organic garden. And one of my funniest memories is the annual turkey harvesting that had a number of us up to our shoulders in 30-pound turkeys, dressing them for freezing.

Behind all the hard work was the basis for our living and working together. We gathered for four "services" a week to speak of our spiritual connection and its application to our lives. It was a tremendous process of being immersed in the One Spirit. I also had invaluable training in public speaking when I participated on numerous occasions as speaker for our many service gatherings. These group opportunities to connect to the One Spirit have stayed with me, much more so than the Emissary principles I learned.

One of the major ways that the Emissaries gave expression to the principles of the organization was through the spiritual technology of Attunement (at one with, in union with) the One Spirit. Attunement is an energy therapy, mostly non-touch, that balances the physiologic and energetic functions of the body. This modality assists the body in finding alignment and union with the One Spirit. All of us at Sunrise participated in receiving attunements as a regular part of our community life. I opted to be trained as one of the attunement practitioners. It was the beginning of my life as a healer, which I felt was a natural part of my Soul's expression. For me, sharing attunement felt like an immense opportunity to be a vessel for spirit, and for me to be a healing blessing to those I was with.

Attunement was also available as an avenue for long-distance, energetic healing. I spent many days holding this attunement vibration for personal and worldwide service. I was right at home transmitting the energy of Divine Love and connection to the people around me, as well as with the visitors who came from all over the world on a regular basis to take part in Emissary classes and conferences. My husband and I even had the honor of traveling to Emissary centers in Africa, Russia, England and France to teach Attunement in the 1980s.

I was very happy and fulfilled in my life and purpose in the Sunrise community. I felt good about all the choices I had made within the context of the Emissary view to know the One Spirit as fully as possible. It was a time of opening to see many avenues of life in a different perspective than the way I had been taught growing up. This was quite natural for my age and the times. This new perspective also related to the exploration of how our sexuality fit in with our spiritual approach.

When my husband and I got married at Sunrise we were asked by one of the couples leading the community if we would like to participate in a more spiritually expanded dynamic in our marriage than just a normal, everyday relationship. Being as service oriented as we both were, we said yes. I went into this realm of exploration because I wanted every aspect of my life to have meaning. I wanted to evolve spiritually. Some part of me thrived on a sense of living outside the box. Specifically, this expanded marriage concept entailed my husband's sexual relationships with selected single women for the purpose of "enfoldment." This enfoldment allowed the single women to have a safe connection with God through husbands who had proven themselves to have a substantial connection to God and the ordained Emissary leadership.

Since then I have discovered that we were not alone as a community during the '70s and '80s in exploring expanded options for sexual relatedness, all in the name of God. Historically, bringing the forces of spirituality and sexuality together in sacred union has been a maze of mistranslations and concepts that have even brought down civilizations. The Emissary program was filled with their own belief systems based on the desire to bring sexuality into the field of spirituality. Exploring new territory can certainly broaden horizons, while at the same time there can be harmful side effects. In the case of my husband and me there was very open communication about who he was with and when. I felt very special in this role, as did he. I was honored by the women involved for being capable of sharing my husband for spiritual purposes. I was among the elite, after all. I was also living under the premise that, since my childhood, the only way for me to get love was to take care of others and their needs first.

It looked as though I was having a very easy, gracious time with the arrangement. We were taught that when a negative feeling came up we were to insert the platitude, "I am not my feelings." We should then transcend the feelings and have a more positive, spiritual attitude, even if it meant faking it or simply suppressing the feeling. Since there was no room given for feelings, I couldn't use them as a natural barometer for how my outer world actually registered to my inner reality. My own heart and Soul perception of the matter were not given credence. I was to stay attuned with the dictates of the spiritual guidelines agreed upon. I was certainly retreating from listening to my own inner wisdom because I was seeing anything I felt or perceived to be in the category of that which needed to be transcended so that the spiritual vision was honored. Also, I was loved and accepted only if my expression was in line with the Emissary "tone," as the leaders of the community defined it. This was a classic example of the way I lived out my own wound of separation. For me, I complied with spiritual principles to know love because my heart was wounded, believing it was not possible to feel the authentic, intimate love with a partner that I desired in this life. It was also natural to me to hold back my heart's expression to make sure that others were taken care of.

My husband loved me as best he knew how while staying aligned first and foremost with the purposes of the community that did not particularly endorse developing a depth of emotional intimacy in marriage. We shared a deep spiritual bond but that did not mean we knew how to be our rich, authentic selves together. This suited me just fine on the emotional level. I could keep my heart protected while being of service and helping others meet their spiritual needs. Or so it seemed...

Then, one day, about ten years into this pattern of extended marriage, the dam broke and my heart could not stay shut off anymore. I was taking a walk with a friend on a beautiful summer day. We stopped by a pine tree to hang out for a moment and enjoy the Colorado sunshine. My dear friend, on whom I counted to "shoot from the hip," asked me how I was doing with all these women spending sexual time with my husband. These affairs were never spoken about outside the circle of those involved. I was taken off guard and immediately went into an elaborate monologue about how great it all was and how special and honored I felt. When I finally stopped my rambling speech, my friend simply replied, "Oh."

When we parted ways, I was walking faster and faster, and suddenly I couldn't hold it back any longer. The dam burst and I cried endless buckets of tears. THIS WAS NOT OKAY! I WAS NOT OKAY! AND, NO, IT WAS NOT WORKING FOR ME! I didn't care what all these other women needed. I needed to claim my heart, my Soul and my life—perhaps for the first time. I had given all these qualities of my spirit away so that others might thrive. I had abandoned myself at a Soul level, and I wanted to realize that most intimate connection—with myself. I wanted to hear the voice of my Soul and not everyone else's ideas for me, even if they were in the name of God, seemingly.

Next, the unraveling began. My friend's appearance was like a fairy godmother showing up for me. I knew it was the voice of my Soul pushing at my heart. Hallelujah! To this day I am eternally grateful for that moment on my Soul's journey. My husband and I attempted to reclaim our marriage without the pattern of extended marriage. The damage to our intimacy was too extensive to make it through that tidal wave of change together. While we worked so hard to develop spiritually, we had not created the emotional skills in our lifestyle to keep a healthy foundation for a deeply loving marriage. In the meantime, he had fallen in love with one of the women we were close with, so the tear in the fabric of our togetherness became irreparable

The unraveling began. It was time for many of us in the community to take a deep look at why we were involved in these patterns and not genuinely happy, and then to ask ourselves what we truly wanted, even if it meant a major shake-up in what seemed valuable and satisfying at some level. We even had an expert in the field of ethics come in and help us sort out our collective belief systems. The ethics expert declared that for the spiritual leaders to have such an authoritative say in our sexual lives was a misuse of power. It was time for me to stop letting others play God and listen more intently to what my heart and Soul wanted to bring forth through my life. My heart was crying out to discover what my unique Soul gifts and strengths were outside of a collective guidance system. It was time to listen to my Soul's compass and move into the next chapter of my life. It was time to discover what it meant to truly be an emissary of Light in the world of my own creating. Many in the community saw these shortcomings in the patterns of an authoritarian power structure as well, so we supported each other in leaving the community to find our new lives, while staying connected as friends and confidantes.

It was an excruciating time for me, walking through the fire of divorce and also losing a community life and a worldwide family of 20 years. Leaving was filled with agonizing growing pains mixed with feelings of betrayal, being used and taken advantage of. This shift also triggered my wound of feeling unwanted and unloved. I couldn't put anyone but myself at fault for buying into aspects and shadows of a system that did not honor self-love and self-worth.

Our daughter Courtney was seven at the time of my separation. I was keenly aware that conscious parenting is essential to allow a child to traverse the divorce chasm from a known to a big unknown. The words I had read in a parenting book at the time were emblazoned in my heart: It is who you are, not what you say, that a child hears. A parent who loves life transmits the energy of loving life to their child. This was also the time of the beginning process of separation from the community. In my heart it was vital to walk through my process of dissolution and re-creation, but also to help Courtney hold sacred and joyful all that she had experienced. This perspective was extremely useful for me, as well, because it reminded me continually that the spirit of what I had experienced those 20 years remained to be built on. It was only the immature aspects within me that needed to be transformed in the fire.

My Soul was on course, as it had been when I first came to Sunrise Ranch. Just because I had gotten caught in the maze of extended marriage did not mean that my Soul's radiance had been crushed. It was just something that I bought into along the way that reflected some unresolved wounds within myself, which no longer served me. Now it was time to hold sacred what was true in my heart and Soul and release all that did not ring true. Doing this also allowed my daughter's experience to remain pure. To this day, she holds her experience at Sunrise as precious and valuable to her core. It was a vital part of her Soul's birthing this lifetime.

After leaving Sunrise Ranch, I watched the patterns of separation from my Soul disintegrate in myself, while I witnessed the reunion with my truth entering into every cell in my body with grace and magic. I was provided for on all levels every step of the way of this huge transition. This gave me the knowledge of the reality and potency of divine guidance, and fortitude of spiritual assistance that is continually at hand.

Being a single mom brought to me the opportunity to help my daughter through a huge impasse for both of us that truly allowed my Soul to take me where it knew I needed to be. This time opened a tremendous door in my Soul journey of learning how to assist others in the deepest of ways: at the level of the heart and Soul.

Nine months after my separation from my husband, he went to South Africa for three months. During that time, Courtney developed a deep terror of going to sleep alone. The moment he left the country was the moment the behavior started. I tried everything, from walking around the house with a flashlight to show her there were no "monsters" lurking or anything to fear, to holding her all night long to make sure she felt safe—all to no avail.

In all my inquiries for help from numerous fields the one thing that *did* magically allow her to relax and sleep in her own bed was finding that she had a Soul connection to her dad and his going to South Africa had deeply disturbed it. I learned that her Soul had made an agreement with her father that he would keep her safe and strong. This was at work at a Soul level, not an emotional level. So, when he left, she did not feel anchored or held spiritually. It was torture for me to feel this in her and to have to helplessly watch her be so desperately afraid all of a sudden. I felt exhausted and helpless. Every evening for three months my life revolved around helping her to feel safe and then to sleep with her so she could get through the night.

I took a Soul journey on her behalf, with her Soul's permission, to her Soul-Essence so that she could reclaim this part of her "spiritual warrior," and strength for herself. She reunited with the strength and assurance within herself that are an inherent part of her Soul gifts.

She slept peacefully by herself now. I reminded her before she went to bed that her true safety and security came from her bond to her inner Soul source of strength of connection to the totality of life. This light was never going out. She got it. The pattern shifted and never reoccurred. What a relief. It was a moment of spiritual recognition for me of the depth of impact our relationship to the Soul has on our daily existence.

This experience with my daughter opened me to the field of spiritual psychology. To see this association between Spirit, the Soul and our physical well-being was dramatically impactful for me personally in my Soul journey, and for my sense of life mission. It awakened me to the passion that lay within me to serve in a way that empowered individuals to live from their heart and Soul. My Soul was bringing me the gift of recognition of my purpose—to connect people to the Soul-Essence. When I declared that my life mattered and I was ready to discover what I had to bring, connected to the community of one life that existed everywhere, the doors opened to bring me the circumstance and people who could shine the light on my path of this burgeoning new growth in my Soul's expansion and influence. Out of the ashes of the old chapter, the new was born.

## My Soul's Emergence

There I was, at age 42, moving, becoming a single parent, renting my first house and shopping at a grocery store for the first time since college. Many elements of living out of community were shocking and frightening, but I felt strongly that it was my time to listen to my Soul's compass and discover what I was made of. I was done selling my Soul for my family of origin, my spiritual community and others needs. It was time to stop disregarding my physical and emotional self so that the One Spirit could truly move through my body, mind and heart, guided by the voice of my Soul. It took courage and a vulnerability that I had never accessed. I was forced to develop my inner resources to find my way in this new world. I was a single parent and I felt like an 18 year old just leaving home for the first time, without the backing of the sense of home and family I had created during my community years. Jumping off a cliff—yes! Freeing and filled with self-discovery—thankfully so!

This time of self-discovery from the inside out also naturally propelled me to develop my gift of healing. It was no accident that I met a wonderful female mentor named Vanessa Rahlston. She became a strong element in the bridge I was building between the life of community I was leaving behind and the new life for myself I was shaping. She opened the door for me to learn how to work with clients, and myself, at a Soul level. Her work had an extensive influence on the topic of my first book, *Soul Mastery: Accessing the Gifts of Your Soul.*

I found myself naturally building on the energetic healing level of Attunement that I had been involved in for the past 20 years. I had graduated from the University of Colorado with a Psychology and Behavioral Biology degree. I was now drawn to take Alchemical Hypnotherapy Training, learn Body Alignment Technique, and get my certification in Cellular Release Therapy. All of this took place as I was transitioning to live alone with my daughter in Boulder, Colorado.

I was excited to develop my own unique approach to psychotherapy. I combined unlocking emotional patterns and clearing Soul-level patterns with getting clients in touch with their inherent Soul-level resources. I call it psychotherapy for the heart and Soul: intuitive counseling combined with psychotherapy skills.

I felt deeply blessed to have my psychotherapy practice take off within a few months after my arrival in Boulder. It certainly was evidence to me that I was in the right place at the right time. I was becoming aware of a presence of benevolence and magic that was supporting me and helping my life to blossom in little miracle after little miracle.

At the same time, I was awakening to the realization that all our wounds have an emotional root *and* also a spiritual root. I so wanted to heal the emotional wounds of my story and clear the patterns I came in with once and for all. As I worked with my own healing from the level of the Soul, I found that the deep patterns of abandonment, betrayal and feeling unwanted did indeed have roots there. And I needed to reconnect with the resources of my Soul to heal those wounds.

My daughter moved away to go to college just a few years ago and then moved to Los Angeles to further her acting career. At that time I had to take another core step of moving beyond my focus on caretaking love to exploring the deeper dimensions of self-love and intimate connection to Divine Love. There I was, living alone, with no one to take care of. I was forced to listen to my own voice and uncover, at a Soul level, what makes up my true spiritual family, and discover what makes me feel loved and wanted if there is no one or nothing external to take care of and validate me.

These moments brought me back to that original belief, and consequent story, that I was unloved and unwanted from the very beginning. It was essential for me to clear all these patterns to make room, not just for my Soul purpose, but also for my Soul's radiance. I realized early on that to just clear patterns was not enough. I had to reconnect to the exiled facet of my Soul that I had disconnected from. Everything lit up in me to enable me to know and experience how reunion with the Soul heals all the wounds and stories. I have healed the patterns of abandonment and betrayal in myself through this reconnection and I feel deeply loved and wanted in a very genuine way. This process has been a powerful transformation filled with much grace and a magnified sense of purpose.

My true spiritual family is an invisible resource of divine, universal support that I can always count on. As I have incorporated that living, breathing reality into my consciousness, I have attracted friends who are unconditionally supportive and understand all of me. They truly welcome me into their hearts and lives.

My connection with my parents has changed dramatically since that beginning when I had such a sense of lack in relationship to them. My mother passed away when I was 30, which was tragic, but it allowed her strong, assured presence to be with me in spirit so that I could count on her absolutely for a sense of unconditional love and support.

My dad's passing is a wonderful example of a Soul's journey coming to a magical conclusion. One night, three years ago, my dad put his Will out on his desk, in a space that he, without exception, left clear when evening came. He said goodnight to his wife, Vera, told her he loved her and went to bed. In the middle of the night Vera was awakened by one gasping breath from my dad, and he was gone. Remarkable. He willed himself to die and move on. He was done. His quality of life had deteriorated, and on the 24th anniversary of my mother's passing from cancer, he crossed over.

As the minister at his memorial service said so eloquently, "Jack (my dad) asked me hundreds and hundreds of questions about Jesus and God in the last ten years that I knew him. I welcomed those questions. And now Jack has chosen to go to be with Jesus and God directly." Well put. My dad was nothing like that when I was growing up, but in the last ten years of his life I saw his heart open and his Soul coming forward in wonderfully transparent ways.

When I think of either of my parents now, they are together. Not out of need to be together again, but to hold a place as divine parents for their family. For the last three years, they have been a pair of guiding lights in my life, a set of divine parents working for all of our family directly and unconditionally. I've planted a rosebush that carries the essence of their presence and my abiding appreciation for their eternal place in the garden of my home and heart.

I have moved through the sensation of being an orphan and welcomed my deceased parents to be with me in spirit. I can feel their presence holding a space of loving parenting for me from the other side.

All of this has helped me to realize that feeling loved and wanted is an inner task that is up to me to perform. Abandonment and betrayal are also inner Soul issues. If I feel abandoned or betrayed, it points me to the place within myself where I abandoned my connection to Spirit, or I betrayed my connection to my Soul's voice. This connection to Spirit creates an expanded reality of spiritual family in my life that connects me to the spirit of the world community that I so relished in the Emissary context.

My psychotherapy practice, which I began over 15 years ago, includes clients and students from around the United States. I have developed my gifts not only as a Soul-level therapist but also as a teacher through the workshops and Soul Mastery trainings that I have conducted for the past 15 years. My book *Soul Mastery: Accessing the Gifts of Your Soul* has given me an even broader scope of connection to many who love me, and want me to be part of their lives, and love the gifts I bring into this world. My journey to discover my authentic self has given me a deep sense of true family and love; not because I was desperately looking for it, but because I let go and opened myself to receive the connection to the divine nature of Love that is our true home.

I have earned my place of wisdom, knowing and ability to assist others in deeply transformative ways through the practice of listening to the voice of my intuition. I might have called myself a late bloomer because I was in my forties before I truly began using my Soul's talents in an outward, career-oriented way, but in retrospect I see that my whole life has been an evolution of my mission and purpose that I choose to call the spiritual adventure of my life. The Soul's journey is my song and life is my dance.

# Part Two:

## Journeying to Your Soul-Essence

# 5

# THE SOUL'S JOURNEY

One potent and breathtaking way to experience the magic of reconnection to your Soul gifts and purposes is by taking a journey to your Soul-Essence. With each journey, an exquisitely magical, love-filled, and deeply satisfying resource floods into you, bringing exactly what is needed to manifest what your heart and Soul long to experience in life. The resources come straight from the universe to your heart and every cell in your body. This is the secret of manifestation from the Soul. This is the means for bringing the Soul riches to life. Directly connecting with your Soul's abundance is a practice that brings true aliveness to your sense of self and purpose. Fulfilling your Soul's longings becomes as natural as breathing as you become versed at connecting to the resources that the Soul-Essence, connected to everything, everywhere, has in store for you and your life purpose.

The following chapters contain sessions I have had with clients, revealing the many ways in which connection to their Soul-Essence has helped them create in very real, practical ways what they wish to manifest in their lives. They have been able to integrate the profound, expanded magic of the gifts of their Soul-Essence into their simple, everyday ways of life. Through their experiences you can see the secret of deep, Soulful, heartfelt manifestation. This depth of manifestation comes from intimate reunion with their Soul gifts and strengths. As you read the sessions, put yourself fully into them so you can also experience the qualities of Spirit being brought forth. Let the experience dwell in you and open you to the gifts of your own Soul-Essence, which is always present to generously give to you. Reading the following sessions will show you the process of journeying to your Soul-Essence. This will set you up to be able to guide your own journeys, so that whenever you have a feeling of lack or longing you can tap into the resources of your Soul.

You might ask, "How can taking a journey to my Soul-Essence help in everyday life?" In a Soul journey the focus is not on fixing problems or getting rid of old patterns. It is on helping to create the Soulful life that is your purpose and joy for being alive. A journey leads to the expansion and fulfillment that you are longing to know in the area of your life that is in need of reconnection to your Soul-Essence.

For instance, if you desire to be a public speaker, you can spend thousands of dollars and hundreds of hours learning how to speak publicly. Or you can spend weeks visualizing how you would look and feel as the public speaker you desire to be.

Or you can reunite with your Soul resources to connect to the qualities of Spirit important to have as a public speaker: confident, charismatic, successful, powerful, viable, passionate, purposeful, etc. As you reach toward those qualities, which your Soul is already holding, and breathe these qualities of Spirit into your cells and your very core, you can be in touch with a knowing of what it is to be a public speaker.

Or, possibly, you wish to know more inner peace. So you practice stilling your mind, possibly for years, hoping that those qualities simply appear. I have spoken with countless people who have been woefully discouraged by meditations designed simply to still the mind.

Instead of focusing on bringing the mind to stillness in hopes of connecting to more expanded states of being including peace, discover the power inherent in going into your heart and expanding to your

Soul-Essence to touch that abundance. Listen to your Soul's voice by placing your attention on the heart, which connects you to your intuition. Following this voice may not feel completely natural at first. But, as you practice, that "still, small" voice will ring with greater clarity and ease within you, and your inner listening ear will increasingly trust its guidance. As you focus on what you value deep in the core of yourself, the less important things, such as mind chatter, will just effortlessly fall away.

For some people it may seem difficult to believe that they can be led to a place where Soul-Essence exists. As you read through the sessions and become familiar with a Soul journey, you will understand how your Soul can open huge doors for your experience, and how you can become more comfortable trying on that experience for yourself. Your conscious mind will feel a cumulative sense of grace in trusting the Soul to open the doors you have not been able to open merely through intention and feeling. Our culture puts very little stock in the value of the invisible world of Spirit, or the idea that our Soul can truly take us where we long to be. These Soul journeys acknowledge this world and its magnificence and provide a way of making it part of our daily lives, just as it has been for most cultures throughout history.

Each chapter is designed to allow you to go deep into an aspect of your Soul-Essence. The Soul is connected to a boundless presence of All That Is. Out of that boundless existence various qualities of Spirit have been birthed that we aspire to carry and hold within our breath. I invite you to connect with the essence that is drawn forth in each section. Your Soul already contains that essence for you to bask in. This is your golden opportunity to reclaim and merge with that essence of yourself that you have longed to hold. These journeys can be experiences that you can follow, providing the essence that supplies the breadth and depth of your Soul's radiance.

# 6

# TAKING
# A SOUL JOURNEY

There is a written meditation referenced with each session that guided the original client from their present state to the deeper, more expanded space of your Soul-Essence. A full version of the meditation is included at the end of the book. To enhance your Soul-Essence journey, the guided meditation is available on CD at www.SoulMastery.net. I highly recommend using this resource to deepen your communication with your Soul.

## The Process

Your first step is to identify the sense of lack or limitation you are experiencing. You might include identifying where this sensation resides in your body. Feel what you are feeling right now, without judgment. Feeling exactly what is present with you will help you take the next step in this journey of manifesting. As you connect with that feeling, actually be it. Whether you feel fear, anger, lack, helplessness, sadness, confusion, unknowing, take a moment to ponder what it is you truly want to experience that lies beneath the present feeling.

Then ask yourself the question, "What is it I truly want that I don't believe I am able to get from where I am now?" As you find yourself naming what you want, be as emotionally honest as you can. Really get to the heart of the matter. Find out what qualities of experience you are longing for. Go beyond the feeling of what you don't want, or are unhappy with, to the longing you have beneath those sensations of lack or limitation. If you still aren't sure what it is you are going after, don't worry. Know that your Soul is wise in the matter. Be open to its gifts and they will abundantly be given to you as you journey to reunite with them at the level of your Soul's radiance.

Sometimes you may have only a vague sense of what you want. You know you want change or expansion. You want to be doing something meaningful but you don't know what that would look like, so you don't know where to start. You may want to make a significant contribution in your life, but also want prosperity and freedom. Take a moment to feel how it would be not to have these qualities contradict themselves.

Ask yourself what qualities of Spirit those experiences would give you. Ask your heart and Soul to help you open to that level of understanding. With a bit of practice it shouldn't take long for your Soul's voice to start to speak to you at the level you actually want your gifts of Spirit to come from. You will be cued in to thinking in terms of the qualities of Spirit you are wanting rather than what you lack, or what you think you want in the physical world alone.

You may want to find your life purpose, for example. What do you do when you feel you are starting at such a generalized point? The same steps apply. Look at all the wants you have within the framework of what finding your life purpose means to you, and prioritize what matters most to you right now. That will help launch you.

Then follow the meditation, remembering to give those longings and desires to the Divine, or the universe, as you hold your heart open to reunite with your sacred Soul-Essence. Let your Soul and all that you are and the interconnectedness of All That Is take you where you long to go.

You may see metaphors or symbolic pictures, images or colors. The possibilities are infinite. The Soul does not work like your linear brain. It works through your creative imagination. Let whatever is there come in:

impressions, sensations, even what you might deem crazy pictures that you may not initially grasp the meaning of. Our intuition is the avenue for the essence of our Soul. Be open at the level of sensing rather than analyzing.

Your linear mind may want to rush in to question your Soul as it works through your heart and creative imagination, just because it is less familiar territory for you to move in. Resist its temptation to take over.

For instance, one client saw a horse. Then she saw herself riding on the horse, and the horse's breathing got her attention. She then recognized the sensation of breathing as a connection to her own heartbeat. From there, the pieces of the puzzle began to come together for her. If she had stopped herself and questioned why she was seeing a horse, the gift would not have been revealed and might have been lost. When an image appears, ask your heart what that image means to you now.

As with dream interpretation, let yourself *be* with what arises and feel what it means from your heart, not your head. If your heart expands as images come in, you are on track. You do not have to go looking for impressions, allow them to come to you. Trying too hard constricts your Soul's movement. Simply ask from your heart to connect and commune with your Soul-Essence and its gift. Stay in a space of openness and wonder, like an explorer exploring the far reaches of space for the first time.

As you reunite with the powerful ingredient of Spirit bringing its treasure to you, bring that image, symbol, feeling or sensation into your heart. You can use your breath to draw this treasure from your sense of expanded awareness into your heart and body. Feel or see the gift you received on your journey and first breathe that image or feeling down into your heart. You can feel it as a stream of energy, or an image surrounded by Light coming into your heart. You can also create a symbol from your experience that personifies what you gained if what you received was abstract or mostly of a feeling nature. The key is having the gift of the journey held in your heart for you to have and hold. This allows the essence of the journey to have an anchor of reality within your heart and, further, into every cell in your body. This is an essential step in allowing your Soul riches into your life. These riches must become part of your very makeup: your cells, your breath, your feeling perception as you walk through life. After you first feel this new-found joy, freedom, power or Divine Love, you will begin to own it as yours and see it penetrating your life. Then you will know the profound meaning it has for you.

As you transport the gift from your Soul-Essence into your heart, the transformation process begins. Whatever we hold in our heart radiates into the whole world and beyond into the whole universe. Absorb the implications of that statement for yourself, your life and for the collective community of humanity. Yes, it radiates throughout your entire self and body and at the same time radiates throughout the Earth. You become that essence. You, with your radiant Soul-Essence shining forth, are filled with the Light of all creation, supporting the next step in your life that matters most to you, whether it is about abundance of love, power, money, confidence, peace or quality-of-life experience reflected in material objects.

Next, you will bring the energy of your Soul's gift into your whole body. You can continue to breathe the image, symbol or feeling impression into your abdomen and then throughout your whole body. You can follow the longer meditation at the end of the book to help you include these experiential steps of connecting more deeply with what you have brought from your Soul-Essence to help you manifest your Soul's fulfillment in life.

The next step is vital. Whatever your Soul-Essence has given you on your journey, relish it. Let it exist in your awareness, in your heart, in your core. Hold it near and dear to your core as you breathe its symbol into the cells of your body, and therefore develop the sense of knowing from a deep wellspring within you that this Soul gift is *you*. It may take some deliberate attention, but it's worth it. Anything that you are discovering or learning for the first time takes practice. You are replacing old patterns and habits that can slip back into place by default if you aren't deliberately choosing to engage the new Soul resource throughout your day. Visualize that precious symbol, image or impression within your heart. Walk through your life with the sense that this gift of your Soul is leading the way. Let your Soul, and this essence you have just reunited with, take you where you long to be. You will be rewarded a thousand-fold each time you choose your Soul's Light to illuminate your life. You can now live from this new dimension of your expanded, fulfilled self. Then live as you've never allowed yourself to live before! Enjoy not only the journey, but also the magnificent revelation of the brilliance of who you are declaring yourself to be. This process connects you to the secret of manifesting in alignment with All That Is and your Soul-Essence. It is your birthright to have and hold the abundance of your radiant Soul-Essence to ignite your life!

## Anchoring and Sanctifying Your Journey

As you open your heart to the precious nature of your Soul-Essence and its abundant gifts, a vital ingredient to staying aligned with this new aspect you are reuniting with lies in your ability to be a spiritual warrior for your Soul's gifts and truth. To be a spiritual warrior for the resources of your Soul gift that you have just reunited with, you must hold this new treasure sacred. To do this, imagine a picture or impression that can carry the strength of your spiritual warrior aspect. This image you hold in your mind's eye will surround your heart to make sure that what you value is honored and held true. It holds respect as well as love for this Soul gift you have gained to be part of your lifeblood. This spiritual warrior energy is absolutely connected to your Soul and the Divine. This image or energy allows you to release old fears that what you value will not be received or cared for. It is also present to alleviate the need to use protection as your anchor.

When you are connected to your Soul and its gifts, strengths and purposes, you no longer need to protect what dwells in your heart. Protection denotes fear. If you have to protect yourself, it is because you are afraid. If you feel you need to protect your heart or your Soul's gifts, it is because you believe there is something of greater power outside yourself that has the capacity to harm what you hold near and dear. If you surround what you love with a quality of sacred honor and respect, the fear and need for protection falls away. This way allows you to be clear that you will not allow in anything disrespectful or out of alignment with your heart and Soul, but you do not do it out of fear. You do it from a place of the power of true divine connection anchoring and sanctifying what you value.

Another step you may wish to take in anchoring the new resources of your Soul comes through creating an energetic umbilical cord between the expanded space of your Soul-Essence, holding the new treasures of your expanded sense of self and your very body. It is good to bring those resources not only to your heart, but also to what I call your womb space for creation. This is your abdomen, which includes your bellybutton, and for women, this also includes your uterus. This is your womb space for the power of all you create from your Soul. As you build this cord in your mind's eye, it allows you to reestablish your life source coming from a spiritual dimension rather than merely a physical dimension. This reconnection can feel very refreshing, renewing and profound.

*7*

# A Self–Guided Journey: To Live in the Heart of God

*This is an example of a self-guided journey
and what it can bring to you.*

Recently I was taking my own Soul journey. It pertained to a longing to know a greater sense of home. Sometimes that can come up when I am traveling repeatedly, or if there is a change in my landscape of support.

So I took this longing for what I termed home and played with what the quality of Spirit was that I truly wanted. I realized that I wanted a deeper knowing of home base within myself that was permanent and eternal and had a universal base. I held that quality of Spirit that I wished to know and merge with as I took my Soul journey.

The following phrase came to me while I was doing my journey to my Soul-Essence. It touched my whole world. I will never be the same again because of it. It holds an energy of universal home anyone can attune to.

*I live in the heart of God. I rest in the heart of God.*

As I journeyed to the space of my Soul-Essence through the steps of the meditation, this phrase came to me out of nowhere. I took the phrase into my heart and began to breathe it into my whole body. It became a declaration of my Soul that sang through my heart. When I said the phrase out loud my heart pounded with joy.

The word God holds the vibration of positive masculine energy. Pure, positive masculine energy lives within every cell and every life form on this planet. It is this energy that holds absolute connection to the Divine—that which is infinite and eternal. At the human level it is also the energy that commands the connection to the Divine be brought forth into living expression. I live at the heart of absolute connection to All That Is. *I live in the heart of God.*

I took a moment to surround this phrase I had brought into my heart with a Light that carried strength to hold the phrase intact and sacred within me. I felt as though it now lived in me and I could use the strength of my conviction of knowing home base anytime that I felt a bit wobbly about my sense of anchor and connection to the Divine.

I then created an umbilical cord of connection between my womb space for creation and my expanded connection to the universal home that the heart of God meant for me.

You may find greater resonance with another phrase that burns in my heart at times when connection to Divine Love is all that matters for me: *I live in the heart of Divine Love.* This phrase also gives me a feeling of an utter sense of home in the purest, most complete way I know.

*I live in the heart of Divine Love. I am at home in Divine Love.*

Find your phrase that holds such sacred depth of Soul connection for yourself, or use this phrase. Let yourself breathe it in, gently and slowly, until it rests in your heart and then in your very abdomen. Give yourself the gift of sacred union with the largest essence of universal home and home base.

Know that this is the umbilical cord to the Divine, now linked to your very womb space for creation, which will allow you to manifest all that you choose to create, born of the heart of God.

As I have allowed this phrase to permeate my very existence, breathing it into my heart and, therefore, my entire bloodstream, my whole world has transformed. I have stepped into the world on a daily basis with a confidence that all is well, and all is fabulous and magnificently unfolding for each of us. This is Soul radiance.

# Part Three:

## A Collection of Soul Journeys

# 8

# SESSIONS ON MONEY

## Recognizing Money as a Quality of Life

Soul wisdom brings a divine hand to the realm of money. It allows us to reunite with the joy, freedom and peace of mind that comes from the feeling of abundance. The field of money has been filled with struggle and hardship for so many. Money symbolizes much more than any of us could comprehend, yet we continue to try to solve our money problems merely from a linear perspective. Is it working for you?! Most would say that it is not. Money, in truth, represents a beautiful avenue for creation. Sadly, it has also carried a structural belief tied to survival that has held us back from letting it be linked to the spiritual influence of true abundance that resides in the whole universe.

It's important to look more closely at what qualities of Spirit we want to connect with when we say we want more money. Then our Soul can bring us that quality of abundance it knows how to reach and generously give to us. This and the next session provide renewal of your resources so that you can have the wealth in life that Spirit is ready to offer you.

**Marilyn:** What I would like to work with today is the topic of money and abundance. It is something I have struggled with for years. I want more money in my life, as I have needs in this area I can't fulfill.

**Susann:** Tell me what your feeling is about money, or how you look at it in this moment in time.

**Marilyn:** At this moment in time? Very differently than how I used to look at it. I used to see it as something I wanted to run away from because it scared me.

**Susann:** How did it scare you?

**Marilyn:** The whole concept of dealing with money scared me. What it meant, how to deal with it, and how to be smart about it. I was never taught. So it had a lot of emotional charge to it. It still does, but I think I am very much more relaxed about the concept of money and abundance because I know the essence of abundance is with me.

**Susann:** So what is it that helped you in that way?

**Marilyn:** My spiritual evolution and my work. The concept of money as a form of energy force makes sense to me.

**Susann:** It makes it a little more doable if it's just energy.

**Marilyn:** Right. It is not as threatening. I have always had this feeling that I am being taken care of and I always will be taken care of with my needs. Even through all this emotional craziness in my family around money, I have held on to that as a very core belief. It is just a trust that money is there, period.

**Susann:** And at the same time you are holding on to a core belief that you are not a great manifester of money.

**Marilyn:** Yes.

**Susann:** So you feel that being taken care of and having a quality of life that you truly desire are two different things.

**Marilyn:** Yes. Right. I know I have been limiting myself. I have enough, just enough. But the feeling of abundance is missing and it is what I am asking for. It is still a bit confusing to me, the actual doing it, the manifesting of money. I can read about it and how to do it. I can hear people talk about it. But, when I bring it into my own personal realm of experience, I am not quite sure what the next steps are, how to actually create that level of abundance. I'm thinking that it's not so much about my thoughts around the idea of money as it is about being open to gifts, surprises, even miracles, around money. This gets me out of my box.

**Susann:** Great.

**Marilyn:** It is refreshing not to feel that I have to actually think up some incredible way of earning money. I have to believe that it is coming and I just have to stay open to whatever I am about to receive.

**Susann:** So receiving is a big piece of it, being open and available and receptive to abundance, rather than saying, "I just have to work harder, longer, more hours, charge more, etc."

**Marilyn:** Yes, that is my legacy, to work harder to earn more money.

**Susann:** So, when you think of your money problems, is it your ability to bring in money that creates the feeling of limitation? Or that when you get money, do you spend it and find you can't save it?

**Marilyn:** I think the problem lies with the amount of money I give away. I am highly generous with others. I still support my sister and I support my dad, a little. I have given money to friends as loans that I have never gotten back. I have supported my son completely through nine years of private school. If you were to look at what I have brought in compared to what has gone out, there is a definite discrepancy. There is a huge amount of overhead in terms of my business. It is crazy. So that is what most of the problem is about.

**Susann:** Thank you for being willing to share that. So, from what you have said earlier, I sense that there is this feeling in you of not wanting to deal with money. As soon as it comes in, it goes out. Generously, but it still goes out. You are not just spending it on stuff. So, even through the filter of generosity, you are still stating, "I don't want to deal with this money, let somebody else deal with it. I will just give it to them."

**Marilyn:** I would like to be able to do other things that are more joyful, fun and playful with the money, even as I share it.

**Susann:** Abundance is a quality of life, in fact. It is a state of being.

Having lots of money doesn't necessarily create an inner feeling of abundance.

**Marilyn:** Absolutely, I don't see abundance as a money thing whatsoever. Money is just a means of having a quality of life.

**Susann:** Wonderful. Describe the qualities of life you would like to be more connected to.

**Marilyn:** Joy and playfulness, much more of a lighthearted lifestyle. Passionate, for sure.

**Susann:** You are a psychiatrist. How do you see your work opening up?

**Marilyn:** I want to move into ways of working with people that are not just strictly that psychiatrist persona, working one-on-one in my little office.

**Susann:** So the joy you wish to know also relates to how you serve the world, the expression of yourself being offered. The expression of yourself in a larger context brings joy for you.

**Marilyn:** I am very service-oriented, and I feel that my work needs to come through my own joy and my own passion.

**Susann:** So there is a combination of being service-oriented and feeling personally, joyfully fulfilled as you are doing that which matters to you. When we are thinking of the money that you are looking for, how do money and joy and service connect?

**Marilyn:** Money is a means to help create all of that.

**Susann:** What I feel we need to do is connect with the aspect of your Soul's essence that knows about creating joy and abundance as you serve in life. Your Soul knows how to use the vehicle of creation that money is. There is something about the spiritual quality of joy and abundance, combining with the physical means of allowing you to serve in a larger capacity in this world, that wants to be known, that feels important. This will help you release the belief that money is something to disrespect or feel bad about.

**Marilyn:** Yes. Part of it is that I grew up in the hippie generation and really was disgusted with corporate America and the whole thing. I was not interested in earning money. I was a student till I was 39 years old. I did not earn money until then, it just didn't mean that much to me.

**Susann:** It had a negative influence to you, also.

**Marilyn:** Yeah, exactly. It was something to pay your bills with and have a fairly comfortable lifestyle with, but other than that it was like, "Yuck!"

**Susann:** So what it feels like we are trying to open up for you now is the knowing that you have a divine right to utilize the systems and values of this world in a whole new way as you receive money for your spiritual expansion and to have a life of greater abundance.

**Marilyn:** Absolutely. Yes. What I have noticed in the last year in particular, is that my fear around money has really diminished. I can say it has almost gone, which is huge.

At this point in my life it is more like, "Oh, God, how do I handle it? What do I do with it? Who do I trust to guide me with it? Who do I trust to help me make money and figure out what to do with the money I have?"

**Susann:** Do you feel you can trust yourself with money?

**Marilyn:** That's a good question to explore.

**Susann:** So let's help you to be able to trust yourself with the resources of life that are brought to you, so that you can be responsible for them, manage them and allow them to create what you want them to create when they are in your hands.

**Marilyn:** That's great.

**Susann:** So let's see what your Soul has to say about what you have always known with respect to money moving through you as an acceptable resource for serving joyously in this world.

**Marilyn:** Okay.

*At this point Susann leads Marilyn in a guided meditation to journey to her Soul-Essence. To follow the meditation for yourself, go to page 229 at the end of the book.*

**Susann:** Let the Light around you move you deeply into the space of your Soul-Essence and knowledge of what it is to create abundance.

**Marilyn:** I have an image of myself in this Shamanic Journey I had in the last year. So it is myself in this other dimension, in an iridescent gown and headdress and just beaming Light. This time I am surrounded by piles of gold, piles around me.

**Susann:** So feel what happens in your physical body right now when you feel that iridescent self surrounded by gold.

**Marilyn:** I just sparkle and it brings a lightness of being that is quite noticeable, and the shift is playful, fun and alive.

**Susann:** So it seems like there is something significant here when you talk about playful, fun and alive. It is like saying, "I am engaging in life. I can do this."

**Marilyn:** Yeah. This is like gliding through life with bells on, just effortless. Ease. Ease.

**Susann:** Good. So stay with it a little more. So in that place where you are iridescent, are you alone? Are you with others?

**Marilyn:** I am alone. When you asked that question, there are some other energies that are starting to appear just as I am coming out of the forest. They are not very well defined. As they come closer they are also laughing and having a good time, and a lot of them have crinkly eyes, a lot of smile lines, sparkly, crinkly, "having lived life" types of faces, but filled with shining joy.

**Susann:** You feel like they have lived life and they are coming back to say that this is what being filled with life feels like.

**Marilyn:** Yeah, like this is the way we all join together. This is the way we connect now because we are all experiencing this. We got it and it is so much different from worrying about everything and struggling so hard. It is like the group is of one mind and Spirit.

**Susann:** They seem very wise. They get it. They are alive, joyful and engaged in life. What would they like to share with you about the value system we call money?

**Marilyn:** This is a hard thing, allowing myself to be a channel. To just let it flow into a channel of allowing. Now I see it as if the gold is raining down. It is always there. It is like spirit. It is always there. It is up to us to receive it.

**Susann:** So it looks like they are helping you to redefine how you see money in this life. It showers down. It is filled with Light. It is filled with ease and joy. It is not this awful thing that evil people work with, as you felt when you were a hippie.

**Marilyn:** It is not awful at all, it is just part of everything else. I don't have a judgment about it. They are telling me another piece of this equation: It is not about whom I trust, in terms of what to do with my money. It is about just opening myself up to allow the right guidance to come in, to know that it is there.

**Susann:** When you are surrounded by these beings, now that you are getting reconnected to this field of clarity, can you trust those who show up?

**Marilyn:** Exactly. (Laugh) I get this sense that this is true retirement, retirement from fear and struggle. Because none of these beings around me, nor myself, are going to stop doing things in the world with others.

**Susann:** So these beings represent you, don't they?

**Marilyn:** Yes. And it is funny because the men have sort of elf clothing on and the women all have gowns on and it is very cozy and beautiful. Maybe a little like those communes originally wanted to be like. Because it is about community too.

**Susann:** What part of it? The joy and abundance part of community?

**Marilyn:** There is just the sharing of it, not so much this is ours and this is yours. It is just such a flow amongst everybody.

**Susann:** Yes. All of your life this is what you wanted money to bring to you. You talked about wanting to expand and have more of a flow instead of being someone who is just sitting rigidly in your office.

**Marilyn:** Yes, because I am so much more, and I have so much more to offer than just being a psychiatrist. There are so many other parts of me that most people don't know and I haven't really allowed myself to express, partly because of the context of this formalized education that I have had. I am pushing the edges of that. It is really the alchemical aspect of it all, the ingredients are coming together more and more.

**Susann:** I am checking about one other piece of this image. Let's bring this community into the Earth plane and let's make sure there is a place here for this wonderful Soul dimension. Let's bring this image that is playful and alive into the Earth and let's see where you want to land as you bring this expanded you with your community of support here.

**Marilyn:** I can see that it is somewhere on the edge of San Francisco. Yeah, somewhere on the edge, just physically.

**Susann:** Does it want to travel around? Does it want to just park?

**Marilyn:** We have landed somewhere out in a field and we are setting up tents. The energy of just being there draws people in. It is not like going out and connecting and doing so much. It is like just making one's presence known and then people getting interested in coming in, like a word of mouth kind of evolution.

**Susann:** And what are people coming in to?

**Marilyn:** They are coming in to find out what is up with us and our iridescence and Light.

**Susann:** How does that enhance your quality of life?

**Marilyn:** Again, it seeds my desire to share more and to do it wholeheartedly, without feeling like I have to stay within certain rules, to do it appropriately with people. We can still dance, or move, or we can do shamanic ritual, or do this or that. That is why I get this stuff about being a gypsy, because now I am free to do what I want, to feel more expansive. People are bringing money with them.

**Susann:** What does money carry for you, when you say that they are bringing money with them?

**Marilyn:** They are appreciative. It's one of the ways they are expressing, "I appreciate what you have and what you are sharing, who you are and what you are giving." So that feels like more of a local beginning. It feels like there is something farther away that I can't quite see. This is less clear, it feels like at some point there is going to be some traveling or some partnering going on with me. Yeah. Absolutely. Some partnering might evolve, and that partnership is part of creating more of the abundance.

**Susann:** The partnership is magnifying the joy, creativity and abundance.

**Marilyn:** Yes, and there is support, I feel supported. My women friends have definitely encouraged me, but the masculine aspect has definitely not been present.

**Susann:** What we are doing today is helping you to extend into yourself and trust the masculine aspect that is there and present within you. These beings are holding that with you now.

**Marilyn:** Yes, and it is a masculine aspect that is very different than the way I have expressed my masculine self for many years, "Get out there and work hard and do that medical thing and be in that world." This is very different. It feels like a real deep support for my masculine aspect so that I don't have to be the masculine.

**Susann:** Right, you can be the feminine, playful and creative self. What you are also looking for is that energy of masculine support, which is very synonymous with money. Masculine energy and money are both a positive energy of support for what you want to create. Masculine energy also stands in appreciation and reward for what you are creating.

In completion, what I want you to do, because we want to see money clearly as a resource for accessing all you want to create, is visualize the actual paper and coin of the physical vehicle of money and see what all of this has to say to you as you see it before you.

**Marilyn:** As the checks or paper money come in, I kiss them and say thank you. I am happy and I bless it and there is no block. There is more joyful connection to it.

**Susann:** Can you feel a sense of loving relationship to it that is naturally a part of you?

**Marilyn:** Yes. It is not work-related.

**Susann:** Good. Money for you is now a stream of Light in paper form. It is available for creating more Light. You can now bring joy and playfulness into the realm of money. I would remind you to be really conscious when you use money and notice how you exchange it and how you relate to it. Continue to visualize yourself, the illumined one, surrounded with gold, with this community in the field, so it is connected with the Earth plane.

What you have just reconnected with is a Soul intention for the creation of abundance in your life. So, each time you re-create these images, you are communicating from your Soul to your conscious and subconscious mind that this special place is where you live. You, the illumined one, surrounded with gold, know how to abundantly create joy, playfulness and expansion of influence. And you value immensely the money that provides this quality of life that your Soul knows.

**Marilyn:** My body is tingling with this new recognition. Thank you.

## Allowing Money to Give You the Power to Create

Money and the topic of manifestation seem to go hand in glove for many. It seems that if we are capable of creating money in our lives we are good at manifesting. And, if we are not good at generating physical funds in our lives, then we aren't so great at manifesting. As I described in the earlier chapters, manifesting is much bigger than intention and focus at the physical level. To manifest something, even physical acquisitions, requires being able to connect with the qualities of Spirit one truly desires.

The following session describes the process in far greater detail.

**Susann:** My understanding is that today we want to work with the manifestation of money in your life. What I want to bring into this time is your connection to an even deeper dimension within yourself to the field of manifestation that your Soul is already fully in touch with and operating from. To truly create what we want to manifest, we have to be connected to the spiritual dimensions from which it comes. What we want to explore, to start with, is the consciousness around what money symbolizes for you. Everyone is just a little different. When one person says, "I want more money in my life," what they are saying is they want freedom. Another person is saying, "I want a higher quality of life."

Everyone has a different view of what wanting money means for them. So we want to focus on what the quality of Spirit is that you really want money to reflect for you, and then we can connect to that quality of Spirit and allow it to flow through you. Then you can embody that quality and allow it to be reflected in the money that you want, to be able to have what it is that you are really looking for in this world. I would love to hear from you what money carries for you.

**Alex:** Yes, I really want to bust some old paradigms and get my show on the road with money.

**Susann:** Let's do it! I suspect that what keeps you from feeling abundant with money is your disconnection to the power to manifest whatever it is that having more money means to you.

**Alex:** What I have noticed is that there are parts of me that are blocking the receiving of money. But I know that it is fully possible to create money in my life. At the same time I feel there are parts of me that are sabotaging me from having a good, healthy relationship with money. There is an immense frustration in me because I see all these gifts and talents that I have, and occasions when I want to bring forth more of myself and help people, and I feel because this lack of the resource of money I can't bring more of these gifts forward. I want more than just a joyful life. There are things that I want to do. I want to be of greater service. Oh, and now I feel my fear of working myself to death. That might be overstating it. Maybe it's more accurate to say I'm afraid of not having enough time for myself, because of working all the time.

**Susann:** So what I hear you are saying is that the fear of "working yourself to death" is creating a block that keeps you from being able to do what you want. You are afraid if you start creating more, you will have to work harder and then you will lose the joy of life.

**Alex:** Yeah, and I want to stay free from this pattern. I saw my father work all the time and he was always unhappy. He was not a happy man.

**Susann:** "Why would I want to have money if I am going to have to work harder and not really live?" Right?

**Alex:** Yes. There is also some type of remembrance that I did something wrong with money. Like screwing some people, or some people died because of what I did. Maybe I ruined a lot of people by misusing my money. And, sometimes, I was really greedy with my money, and yet I was also really loving and giving at the same time. Other times, I misused money and it's almost like I made an oath in some lifetime, or even a couple of lifetimes. I was so powerful, and I said at the time that I would never do that again and use money or wealth in that way.

**Susann:** Okay. So money for you is equated with wealth. And I would also like to bring in the word "power." You misused your power. You had resources given to you, which were a form of money. Whether it was in the form of gold coins, or actual bills, or property, we don't know, but you misused that power which was given to you.

**Alex:** Yes, that feels like the core right there.

**Susann:** So let's go back to that feeling you have when you want to create and manifest more money. What does having money mean to you?

**Alex:** The first word that comes up is power. I feel that power. When I say money or power, they are more than words. I want to go in a new direction as it relates to power and money. I feel there is something in me keeping me from going there, from rising to the occasion.

**Susann:** So you want to create a new definition of power and money for yourself. And you are feeling that there is a block keeping you from doing that. Okay. I want to bring forward my gifts but this block is in the way because it involves expanding, being more powerful, having money, and that means it can become bad. So, in order to release that block, we have to get in touch with the true essence of power in you. For you, money seems to be equated with power. We want now to connect you with your Soul-Essence place that knows the true dynamic of power. We want you to feel how your power is connected to a universal energy source that continually feeds truthful power to you from which to manifest that which you long to create. We want you to see and remember what it feels like to have that true sense of power, and then be able to have money be a reflection of that in your world. How does that resonate with you?

**Alex:** Good.

**Susann:** Let me ask you, if you did have this money, what do you see yourself using it for? How would it serve you?

**Alex:** I want to build a huge healing center for people.

**Susann:** You want to provide a huge healing center for people, and it feels like you need the power to do that.

**Alex:** Most definitely. I need my entire divinity to be able to do that. Maybe that is an overstatement, but I don't think so. I want to be able to bring that into manifestation.

**Susann:** Right, I would agree with you in that regard, that in order for anyone to expand into the world more freely we have to expand our connection to the Divine as the power source to fuel what it is we want to create in the world.

**Alex:** Travel. I want to go all around the world.

**Susann:** What is the usefulness of travel for you?

**Alex:** Travel allows me to reach more people.

**Susann:** In what way?

**Alex:** By giving workshops and trainings in the talents I have.

**Susann:** You want to be able to expose yourself and your gifts to more people, but you can't because you are feeling like you lack the money and power to do so.

**Alex:** Yes, and what my heart and Soul really want to do is go to really impoverished villages and live there, so I can provide for them and help them, and not just with the trainings. I want to help my friends when they are in need, helping them with money. I also want to help homeless people. Not just by giving them money, but also by giving them resources that will help them expand their lives and get out of their situation.

**Susann:** Wonderful. Let's talk about the resources that you want to give them. What I am hearing from you is that you want to have greater power primarily, and money is a reflection of that. And you are also saying that you want to help empower other people. Just giving them money because you feel sorry for them is a powerless act. So what you are saying is that you want to feel divinely powerful and utilize the resource of money to help others feel more powerful, by sharing the wealth of what it feels like to be in your true divine power.

**Alex:** Yes, mainly I want to serve people and I want to help people to grow.

**Susann:** You want to expand your ability to have what you need to create that. Money is a tool and there is nothing wrong with acknowledging that. It is the medium of exchange that we have. What we want to do is connect you to your Soul's knowing of what it is to hold that true power and purpose that will serve you and those you wish to serve. So we are going to take you on a journey to connect with the Soul-Essence within you that knows how to hold this power in a way that serves the Divine, and serves you at the same time. It is all connected.

*At this point Susann leads Alex in a guided meditation to journey to his Soul-Essence. To follow the meditation for yourself, go to page 229 at the end of the book.*

**Susann:** So I would like you now to connect with that place of your Soul-Essence that knows what it is to hold pure connection to the universal power that fuels your Soul. Feel what it is to move to that connection. If you choose to, share with me what it's like to be in that place that your Soul is bringing you to.

**Alex:** It feels like this is a dimension I have not been to in a long while. I feel like I am being reintegrated into this dimension. It feels almost tangible. It's not a room, not even a bubble, just a space. The word that came up is "reborn," being reborn. The question my mind has is, "What do I do with this?"

**Susann:** Okay, I can help you with that. It feels like you want to be reborn because you want to come into life differently.

**Alex:** And there is a past life that came through. A past life in which I was paid money and I sold out my village and my people and the village burned. That is what came up in the beginning of my meditation. So it is like a rebirth and dissolving of karma and letting go of past things and moving into a space of truth and Divine power and what is real and what is true. Yeah.

**Susann:** What resources do you need right now to bring you the power you need to experience this rebirth?

**Alex:** Safety, softness, being held and embraced but not constricted, knowing that everything is going to be okay. Permission—that's interesting—permission to exist in this new way.

**Susann:** How can you create those in this dimension?

**Alex:** Acceptance, choice, surrender.

**Susann:** Let's create those qualities for you through an image. Let's see it as a womb space for your birth, which has those qualities for your rebirth within it. What would that womb space look like?

**Alex:** The beating of a heart.

**Susann:** Would that be a universal heartbeat, or an anatomical heartbeat?

**Alex:** More personal. The heartbeat of my own being. I need this womb space to be bigger, all-inclusive. And at the same time I feel like I need to be in the womb a little bit longer.

**Susann:** This relates to choice. You get to choose the nature of your womb. You choose what the nature of your connection to universal power is.

**Alex:** Okay. I am connected to the source of All That Is. I feel safe, nourished. Everything I need in any given moment is pumping into me. So powerful.

**Susann:** Do you feel that, see that, or is it just a vague impression?

**Alex:** There is an expansion happening now, it is like the birth of the universe. New choices. There is no end to that. I can let it expand as far as I want it to.

**Susann:** Is there a sense of infinity to it? Is it the universe you are creating?

**Alex:** Yes, I am feeling layers of the infinity within me. I have Light. What is the body of Light that surrounds me?

**Susann:** Remember you talked about the qualities you wanted to have surrounding you while you were rebirthing yourself? It feels like the body of Light around you is holding all those frequencies you described.

**Alex:** Right.

**Susann:** Let's feel the power of this creation occurring within you and around you at this moment. You are birthing this infinite source, this power of a universal nature. What I want you to do is feel how this relates to the physical reality that you are getting ready to birth for yourself here. Feel how it brings you the power you are looking for to expand in the way you wish to. The foundation of power is what you are birthing within yourself.

**Alex:** What is coming up is the sight of things that I want to create: my dreams and desires. They are like balls and masses of energy. I am able to expand that as I expand my universe of self.

**Susann:** There is no limit to that which you dream of and wish to create. Connecting, expanding, feeding and accepting. One of the blocks you had was the feeling of the limitations of this world. You used to feel that you could have connection to the universal dimension while you were out in the universe, but you could not have a connection to the universal dimension while you were here in this world, in your physical sense of self.

**Alex:** Yes, that is what it felt like.

**Susann:** You were feeling that if you created these things that mattered so much to you it would mean hard work, and hard work leads to unhappiness. Now feel what it is like to be that infinitely power-filled self.

**Alex:** Yes, I'm not so involved with what I do, but where I come from.

**Susann:** What about the misuse of money, wealth and power? How does that sit with you now?

**Alex:** Good question. The phrase I want to use about all that now is "not relevant."

**Susann:** The misuse of power is irrelevant in this space.

**Alex:** It is just not there. It is not necessary. There is such purity in this space with my body and my cells. This new space growing inside me now cannot hold fear.

**Susann:** And money? You came today with the idea that you would like to have more money. How do you see the idea of having more money now, from this new space?

**Alex:** I am "reformatting" now. Oh, good. Okay. So now what I am doing is trying to go into the true essence of money. I am feeling the true energy of money is the essence of creation. I see the money and the bills. I see paper money and the coins and at its very center I see the pure energy of creation. Oh, God, I used not to want or let my money even touch me—now I am trying to accept what I am doing with money. I am letting my umbilical cord connect with the true creative essence of money and be one with the true essence of my body, which I wouldn't dare do in the past. I will let that happen now. I see now that I can be a magnet to money because I am carrying that frequency. And, beyond that, I am a magnet for creative energy on many different levels.

**Susann:** May you let yourself be an open vehicle to receive that precious creative energy to be used for the abundance of your expression of life. May you receive the money you wish for to reflect your expanded, universal connection to the true source of power that you are.

**Alex:** I just want to be in my body now and to just be here and create from this powerful, pure space that I'm holding in my body, which knows how to relate to money in a good way, for service, for assisting others. Big reframe.

**Susann:** Excellent.

**Alex:** Thank you so much. I feel very full of Light and full of unlimited possibilities. I can go with this.

# 9

# SESSIONS ON POWER

## Being in Command of My Life

So often we may feel helpless, overwhelmed and filled with the sensation that something outside ourselves is in charge of us and our life. We may feel victim to a force we feel we cannot control. This can make us feel imprisoned or misunderstood or that no one can fill our endless needs. Sound familiar, even in a smaller degree than I have just described? Coming back to feeling in command of our life is as simple as getting reconnected to the source of true power that animates our life, allowing it to ignite our Soul strengths. Here is an example of that process.

**Rita:** Okay, I want this reading/healing to help with releasing any energy that prevents me from owning my own space physically, spiritually, emotionally and more.

**Susann:** I like the "more."

**Rita:** Well, I want to have lots of options. I also feel nervous about taking a journey to my Soul-Essence. I guess because I have difficulty owning my space here I'm nervous that I'll have difficulty owning my Soul. Maybe I'm scared that it won't be there, or I won't be allowed to have it, or it might be taken from me. What an awful thought.

**Susann:** This is so good that you are uncovering these feelings and bringing them to the surface. I will help you feel safe to travel to your Soul-Essence on your terms. I suspect, from what you are saying, that the root of your problem lies at a Soul level, in fact. As we resolve it there it will translate into the physical world here quite naturally.

**Rita:** Since I am from France, when I came here to this country I was given the label "alien" citizen. Pretty funny. I feel like an alien often, so it doesn't bother me to be given that label. I feel so much unhappy energy in people around me. And I am a happy person. So, when I feel that energy in my space, I go out of happy to try to help them. Then I get plugged up and I am not happy, and I end up going home and having a fight with my husband for a stupid thing. So I remembered what I read in your book (*Soul Mastery: Accessing the Gifts of Your Soul*), and I thought about being more true to the Light that I am. Because I'm in transition in my physical life I was not sure how to hold that Light. Now I feel like I'm almost a light bulb, and now I attract attention.

**Susann:** And that gets scary, doesn't it?

**Rita:** Yeah, and, honestly, since I was young, my intention and my thought has been to serve God in Divine Love and in Light. It's always been that when I connect with divine energy I can uplift myself and people around me, and I know this is my purpose. I know that's what serves me. I know what you bring can help me, but what do I do now?

**Susann:** Yes, I am happy to help you with this. What I hear from you is the concern that if you open yourself up too much and start to be freely available with your Light, something will come and take it from you and harm you for it. So everything in you wants to get reconnected to Divine Love and create your own space based on Light, and at the same time, there are these unconscious fears that say, "Yes, but when I really expand and I'm a light bulb of Divine Love, this is when they take that from me!" You don't trust yourself living from your Soul-Essence that is birthed from Light. That's all. It's not about anyone else. It is your time to discover and remember how to hold your authentic Light-filled self and trust that this is not only possible, but is, in fact, all that matters. As long as you are in command of holding that Light in yourself, no one can harm that.

Let's help you remember how to be in command of your life and your space and know that being a light bulb only magnifies Light and doesn't attract negative attention. When you leave your space of Light, that's when you get in trouble. Your subconscious holds a feeling that you're the "alien," and these people here in this world are in command and there's nothing you can do but try to control the outer situation. What we're reorienting in you is a feeling of remembrance that being in command is truly being connected to your Soul-Essence, which is already connected to the Divine. So it's very good that you're saying, "I want to be in command of my own space." That is the key. And just a little deeper than that is the command to your world, "I want to make sure that Divine Love and Light is in my space, first and foremost. I'm not so concerned about whether love gets to all these other people. My job and purpose really is to bring Light into my space, and when Light is here, it's everywhere!"

**Rita:** I agree.

**Susann:** You put out energy of trying to transform others to get them out of their pain into the frequency of Light. At a Soul level it's natural to do this, but not at your own expense.

**Rita:** You know, I've been told that I tend to try to fill people's needs by giving them everything I have. My life brings me, because of my massage work, a lot of people with pain. All day long. I feel their expectations, and I feel that their needs have not been met. I do my best and feel like I'm not doing enough because they don't want to open up, or I can feel whatever they have that keeps them closed or not open to receive. And I do struggle because I try to stay neutral and give the best that I can. But I do see myself not changing their state of pain and then starting to judge myself. What did I do wrong? It gets crazy and goes nowhere. So how can we move this pattern?

**Susann:** To start with I want you to see that staying neutral doesn't serve you. For you, it feels like staying neutral is really stepping outside of yourself and not being in command of the frequency you choose to hold. In a neutral space, you are, in fact, inviting others to drop their pain or problems into your open "neutral" field. Instead of being neutral, what you want to be is exquisitely connected. You want to be so connected that you are more in the space of Divine Love and Light than you are in this world, functioning in the space of trying very hard, overworking, to try to get rid of other's pain all by yourself.

In that self-created space of trying to fix others, you have abandoned your exquisite connection to Light that is your true food source, without the tremendous support your connection to Light gives you. Do you see what I mean? Your job is to be this amazing spiritual being that you are. You want to learn to not overextend yourself into another's space to transform them, or try to control the outer situation. You walk lightly in this world, holding your exquisite Soul connection that matters most to you, while you dance in the field of life that comes to you.

So, if you are applying this to giving a massage, this is how it looks: when a person comes to you, you take into account what they are presenting, in much the same way as I am doing with you now. I am not trying to get rid of your angst or even solve your dilemma with a great technique. I am allowing you to connect with your Soul resources and breathe those into your life situations so you can be more in command of your life from the level of Spirit. Do you see how this applies to you and your massage clients? You are communing deeply with Divine Love, and this person happens to be in your energy field while you're communing with Divine Love. What a gift that is! It is much more of a gift to them than being bothered or worried about their pain or focused on trying to get rid of it.

They came to you to reconnect with life energy in the place where the pain is. And the only way for you to allow them to reconnect with this life energy is for you to be so in communion with Divine Love and Light, which is life energy, that it has an opportunity to move right into their space. When you're neutral, you are open to whatever the dominant vibration is and the dominant vibration would be pain! So your job is to really be in command of your space and hold the energy of Light while you just happen to be rubbing their neck, or whatever. They describe to you what is happening with them, and you put that into the equation, and you let your connection to the healing energy that Light is have its divine way with them where they are open to receive it. No pain, no drain.

**Rita:** Okay.

**Susann:** Does that help?

**Rita:** Ah, energy is moving.

**Susann:** Something in you can relax because instead of being filled with fear about what might come and take what you are from you, you can know that holding love and Light is the answer to all situations.

**Rita:** Hooray! That's simple.

**Susann:** Let us take a journey to the depth of your Soul-Essence that you may be reunited with the rich source of exquisite connection to the true power that allows you to be in command of your life.

*At this point Susann leads Rita in a guided meditation to journey to her Soul-Essence. To follow the meditation for yourself, go to page 229 at the end of the book.*

**Susann:** Take your time and make sure that Light surrounds you at all times as you journey. Make sure you give yourself this support of Light holding sacred all that you are as you travel. Know that as Light surrounds you, it is the only energy that can accompany you on your mission now. What's that like for you as you exist in that dimension?

**Rita:** I'm looking at a lighthouse. That's the type of picture I see. Like darkness but a lot of Light pointing and showing direction.

**Susann:** Does it feel like there are one or two places that you feel directed or compelled to go to in this Light?

**Rita:** I can see one direction showing itself to me. Yes, I can go there. It's like coming out of the darkness, or coming out of a tunnel.

**Susann:** Yes!

**Rita:** I see more variety of colors now. Okay, I'm going into a framelike structure. It's almost like I'm going above the clouds, but I'm beyond the clouds. Ahhh! Good. I'm still ascending to something, I don't know—a kind of a temple, house. It's a sense I have of merging with a sacred space. It's giving me a sense of calm. It's almost like I'm going into a classroom.

**Susann:** Wonderful.

**Rita:** The sense that I have is as if I'm being fed with new information in the classroom. I am merging with a new piece of information at a deeper level.

**Susann:** This is something you can remember to do when you are asking for clarity and direction about something in your daily life. You can ask to connect to this classroom space so you can be given a new piece of information that you aren't getting at this level.

**Rita:** Yes, good. My other sense is that there is a cleanup happening. It's almost like I lift up a kind of layer of energy that doesn't serve me. There's kind of a cleanup scene. I can see this clearing of an old layer occurring. Probably fear. Oh, wow! I see colors now. I can see the classroom space extending. Good. My, my. Wow. Even in my physical state I feel the energy expanding around my space in the room.

**Susann:** It feels like what is occurring is the re-creation of this space that is meant to be the space for your Soul.

**Rita:** Yes. True. It's getting quiet. Almost like an adjustment to this new state with the vibration of movement. Now it's become more like one space, so even my physical body became quiet. It's almost like I'm trying to blend water with oil. The mixing was shaky and now it's become calm.

**Susann:** So it was a feeling like your old vibration and this new vibration didn't quite meld, but then it opened up to be able to merge.

**Rita:** Yes, exactly. It's like being inside a colorful crystal. There's not just one color. It's like being in a space of colors, but they don't really move. That's what I see. This space of colors is my space. I created it. It is the space around me, like a womb space for my Soul. Wow! I get to have it and it feels like a reunion. Remember in *The Wizard of Oz* how the tin man got his heart back and the lion got his courage? I feel like that. I feel like an essential part of me has returned. Ah! This is good.

**Susann:** How does it make you feel to be there?

**Rita:** I feel surrounded in this crystal of colors and it makes me feel strong. Like I have a home and place of support.

**Susann:** Feel that crystal of colors coming into your heart. Let yourself take this strength of connection to your Soul space into yourself. First, through your heart and then breathe it into the rest of your body, like we did in the meditation. Let your breath carry the crystal of colors to all your cells, so this connection can flood in, as all of you is now open to trust it and receive it.

**Rita:** The energy came in a spiral and the word that came up was unity. So it's kind of from above going down to my entire energy field or this whole body.

**Susann:** Nice. So if you want to bring in just a few words that describes what it's like to have that sacred union again with your Soul-Essence, and have union with the Divine Love that exists everywhere and in all things, what would that be?

**Rita:** Very powerful. I do feel I am in command of my life. I feel in charge of how I use my energy field and who comes into it. Very, very good.

**Susann:** Can you feel your ability now to declare this space as your own? Can you declare that you do not want to betray this connection no matter how much pain another is in?

**Rita:** Ah. I have to say that I'm receiving so much and it's so, so, so beautiful. I have to say that it kind of touched the space in me of deserving to receive. Wow, at the same time, yes, I want to receive this.

**Susann:** Wonderful. This is your heart song. "This is what I wish to receive. This is what feeds me." Well, it feels like we want to add to this declaration, "Yes, and this is what gives me life!"

**Rita:** Hmmm. That feels real.

**Susann:** Consider that this space is what helps to create the space of knowing what gives you life rather than thinking that helping someone else is going to give you life.

**Rita:** Okay, yeah. I see that. If I have life others can reach to life, rather than me giving my space, my life, to them.

**Susann:** Consider that universal life opened the door for you to create this sacred Soul space for yourself. It is so beautiful and such a powerful gift you carry. Do you not want to live this same way? You hold this sacred vibration and it opens the door for those around you to create their own space of life, out of pain.

**Rita:** Ahhh! It seems that I'm coming back. Seems like what I was seeing was communion with that energy, and now the picture is that I'm coming back into this world without needing anything.

**Susann:** You are bringing this sacred Soul space with you this time, without creating separation from it in order to be here. You are a unique Soul with an individual expression but you aren't separate from the larger energy field that birthed you. You are in communication with it.

So now take a moment, when you're ready, to feel yourself primarily in this existence. And feel what it would feel like to be with another, either in a healing context or in the context of relationship, and see how you would relate to them while in this sacred space.

**Rita:** I feel like staying connected to this sacred space is all that matters. Wow! I like feeling in charge again. I like feeling like I matter. Others do too, and I am happy to help them, but not at my expense. Okay! I like this power of pure Love I feel.

**Susann:** Wonderful. This is what your Soul is asking you to do. It is asking you to merge with this sacred space. And it helps you with that feeling of not being afraid of any energy that another might carry. You can hold that Divine Love that you are, no matter what. So you are truly in command of your life. Well done.

**Rita:** This is excellent! Look out world—here I come.

# Acknowledging the Power to Be Myself

This session is with a woman I have worked with a number of times. She is, therefore, quite adept at the journey part of our session. A vital part of this session for her is to link the abusive situation she endured in her childhood to the wound of separation from her Soul, and realize that very wound created the abusive situation for her. This separation created a weakness that drew the abuser, hungry to take advantage of her need to be reconnected to a power source she wasn't feeling within herself. We help her reconnect to the only true source of power, which is what I call universal Light, so she can bring that back into her body and feel the strength of connection within herself that did not need the external power source that, in this case, the abuser provided.

When there has been an abusive situation, there are a myriad of ways that one's spirit has been broken. This session and the one entitled "Freedom to Create" cover two facets of the core of the pattern of abuse, addressed at a Soul level.

**Jane:** When I was four years old, my abuser kept blaming me and saying, "It's all your fault. You are such a cute little girl." So what I put together when I was recalling this is the belief that if I am fully who I am, I will attract these awful people and they will abuse me. If I am a wisp of myself then I won't be attractive to others. I have a memory of feeling that I can't trust anyone, and that I have to become less of myself to survive. I'm barely anything and it's still dangerous. Then I realized that since I didn't trust anyone I had to become the responsible one, working hard to keep myself together.

**Susann:** So, in essence, you had to work hard to stay responsible for your own life, your own sense of self, so no one would take it.

**Jane:** Yes, and I realized that if I was my bright self, I would be abused for that. So it was smart not to be so bright a Light. I remember being very bright as a baby, but it wasn't okay to maintain that brilliance, and so it was better to shut it down. My source of brightness came from my connection to Source, so I'd better cut that off. That seems to be what happened, I believe.

**Susann:** That feels very accurate. This is the root of so many scenarios of abuse, which reminds me, once again, that the core of every wound is the wound of separation from the Soul.

**Jane:** So, by being less of myself, I was being even more susceptible because I was disconnected from my true power source, which made me like a weakened prey or the runt of the litter.

**Susann:** Yet you thought you were helping yourself out by dimming your Light.

**Jane:** I did think I was helping myself out. But now I don't want to dim my Light anymore. I want to feel the strength of being fully alive. I have missed giving myself permission to do that.

When I think of being fully alive I feel my four-year-old self getting very scared because I couldn't stop the abuser. I need help in remembering how to feel fully alive and safe to be myself. I feel helplessness taking over, and "Why me?" and "Why didn't God or the universe help me?"

**Susann:** You couldn't imagine how you could have placed yourself in this situation. The key is replacing the sense of helplessness and hopelessness that makes you collapse.

**Jane:** Right now I can't imagine digging myself out of that hole in relationship to the abuse.

**Susann:** That is why we want to draw on your Soul resources to dig you out and give you a higher perspective, so that your Soul can help you reunite with the inherent strength and courage your Soul's connection to Light naturally gives you. I will remind you that the Light is too hot to handle, so to speak. Abusers will find the weakness in you and go after it, not the strength. When you hold that unwavering connection to the source of your inherent strength, you feel infallible, not helpless. When you are in love, you feel that nothing can harm you. You are filled with the strength of your heart's openness and radiance

**Jane:** I'm not sure why I can't get in touch with my anger around all of this.

**Susann:** Often we equate showing our anger with having to show up more fully in the situation that makes us uncomfortable to start with. If you get angry, you are moving out of your "wisp of self" smallness that says, "Don't look at me." Anger can be used as a means of moving out of helplessness into regaining your inherent sense of power. For you it is a way to reclaim yourself and the fact that your life matters. "You cannot have my lifeblood," is a way of declaring that you are in command of your natural power. Your fear of giving your lifeblood expression, which might show up as your fear of being angry, stems from your fear of shining brightly. Also, those who abuse you are misusing their power. So you don't develop a very healthy association with power.

**Jane:** I certainly didn't want to be anything like them.

**Susann:** That's true. So you had another reason, as you perceived it from the vantage point of a small child, not to trust power and therefore not to give it expression yourself.

**Jane:** So my thoughts are going back to this realization I had that if I remain less connected to Source and my Soul-Essence, then I will be less attractive and they will leave me alone. How do I reclaim my connection to Source and my Soul without being terrified it will just be taken from me again?

**Susann:** I understand the feeling you carried from a child's perspective that it doesn't matter how strong your connection is, the physical, adult power of the abuser is always stronger. What we want to help you remember is that to be connected means the power is with you. You and your Soul are connected to an infinite field of power, wisdom, community, support and foundational love. It isn't just "little girl you" against "big man abuser." Remember, the abuser's radar is on your weakness, and the weakness stems from the disconnection you hold. When you are solidly connected in your Soul and self you aren't a viable target.

**Jane:** Another problem I have is that I am not inspired to create anything because I don't feel connected to a larger field of purpose for creating. I don't feel supported or inspired.

**Susann:** If you aren't feeling the joy of being connected to a sense of larger support and purpose, all you have left is a superficial reason to do something. For you, this is not enough of a reason to create. Also, when you only have a superficial reason to do something, or to just live, you will often have the tendency to buy into someone else's purposes. Those purposes result in that person using you to get their need for power met. They take advantage of you in order to feel a sense of power over you so they can consume your life force. As a child you had lots of that!

**Jane:** I remember my abuser giving me attention, first and foremost. I was hungry for attention and the feeling of being taken care of. To feed off my attention made them feel powerful. Wow! Then the game is on. We are equals on the playing field of need. Yuck. How do I get off that playing field for good?

**Susann:** Here we go! We want to allow you to reclaim the true sense of power that comes from absolute connection to universal Light, and thus the feeling of great aliveness coursing through your body, and your sense of creativity. This is the feeling of adventure you were seeking when you encountered those who wanted to take advantage of your aliveness. Your Soul holds that true sense of the adventure of life you can carry within yourself, so you don't have to get in trouble seeking it through others. I have no doubt that you can feel and reunite with that sense of freedom to create again.

**Jane:** That would be such a relief.

**Susann:** The joy of adventure is synonymous with experiencing connection to your true self and having the confidence to live from that unique self.

**Jane:** It's like having Source come through you and then choosing what you want to create from that powerful, assured place.

**Susann:** That's what we want you to experience again in your life now. It is your divine legacy.

*At this point Susann leads Jane in a guided meditation to journey to her Soul-Essence. To follow the meditation for yourself, go to page 229 at the end of the book.*

❧

**Susann:** Fill yourself from the top of your head to the tips of your toes with that abundant universal Light.

**Jane:** As I filled myself with Light and tried to connect it to the feeling of the joy of creation, I got stuck because I had the feeling that I knew I would get hurt if I tried to do that anymore.

**Susann:** As you surround yourself with Light, hold that awareness of what you were just describing. Now feel your fear of being hurt. Let the Light surround that feeling of fear within you as well.

**Jane:** Okay. I can do that now. That's better.

**Susann:** So, as you travel as Light to the place of your Soul-Essence, allow yourself to open to seeing, sensing, feeling and knowing in yourself what is happening in that space around you and within you.

**Jane:** I see myself surrounded in a brilliant, soft, warm light, and see many angelic beings with me.

**Susann:** Sense what the angelic presence is for you. Why has it come in to be with you?

**Jane:** It feels like that presence is there to support me in my connection to Source and my Soul. It's strength, actually.

**Susann:** Let yourself breathe in that support and feel how it does strengthen you, in fact.

**Jane:** Okay…I like that. I didn't mention it before, but when the Light and angels were present there was also darkness in the background that I was aware of. As I breathed in the Light and support and I got larger, the dark, which looks black, got smaller. The sense of community is there, which I like.

**Susann:** Excellent, Jane. You're doing great.

**Jane:** Now I feel a hesitancy to create. I'm not sure about creating and I'm not sure who I am. I'm tentative. I want to feel more confidence that this is where I need to be. Do I belong here? Do I have the power to be myself, freely?

**Susann:** Let's go back to that moment that you said you got larger. Ask yourself what allowed you to get larger.

**Jane:** I was in that place of the power of creation. Yeah. And I let myself be there so it could keep growing.

**Susann:** You were fueled by the connection. Is that true?

**Jane:** Yes. I grew because I knew I was in the right place. Then I got funny about what I wanted to create. Sort of like going into my head to figure out the best thing to create, rather than just staying connected and let that fuel what gets created. I get that. I'll try that right now.

**Susann:** As you are connected and breathing in that Source connection, your Soul co-creates with Source. There is no blind trust involved. Blind trust opens the door to trust people who aren't aligned with Source to come into your creative field. Only those who are on your wavelength can be with you.

**Jane:** I want to bottle this connection so I don't lose it.

**Susann:** Okay. I would be happy to describe to you how to create that. First, bring your awareness to that sense of connection you felt to the brilliant, warm, soft Light surrounding you, accompanied by the presence of the angels as you felt it. Now put all your attention on your breath. Then go back to putting attention on the presence of Light. Then put all your attention on your breath. As you go back and forth with this, you will be drawing that awareness into your breath that goes deeper each time, allowing you to fill your body with that Light presence. Keep going until you feel that essence in yourself. You have bottled it. You are the genie of Light in the bottle of your body.

**Jane:** This allows me to feel joy and adventure in my body. I am not looking outward for adventure and joy, but my inner flame of connection fuels it.

**Susann:** This is your genuine means of holding power that no one can take from you. You aren't unconsciously asking someone to hold a source of power and adventure for you because you are feeling empty and helpless to know how to fill that emptiness, without knowing why. Or without understanding why you would attract someone who misuses power.

**Jane:** I feel so relieved to have a new way of operating. I can get the connection and support I have been looking for and breathe that in and not be afraid I will be hurt for it, or it will be taken from me. Amazing.

**Susann:** You could say that your Soul is happy to be present with you more fully to fill those places that were empty before, and to give you "food" that you can really trust. True Soul food. This is much better than getting candy from a stranger or attention from someone who isn't part of your support structure.

**Jane:** As you were speaking, I was breathing my Soul's happiness in and I feel tears of joy for the reunion. I also feel a resolve around those abusive situations from my childhood that I never felt before. And we didn't even have to go back to those horrible times to relive and rectify them.

**Susann:** Your Soul has the wisdom to give you what you were truly hungering for. Enjoy the banquet!

**Jane:** I am! Thank you!

# 10

# SESSIONS ON LOVE

## Getting to Higher Love

Wouldn't it be great if your heart were fully available to love freely? Compare that to the state most of us live in, which uses the inherent richness of our heart to make sure we are safe and taken care of. It may not be something we are consciously aware of, but I have certainly noticed in my many years of working with people of all ages that a majority of our relationships are based on the need to be taken care of. This need could show itself in our expectations around our parents, our children, our spouses and even our coworkers. We end up using our heart to make sure we are taken care of, rather than using it for its divine purpose. The heart is the window through which our Soul can shine its expression of Divine Love.

Often we fall in love while holding an overlying hope that our need to be taken care of will be fulfilled by our partner. These kinds of expectations set us up for the disappointment that comes when a partner cannot meet those needs sufficiently. Even our friendships can be laced with a feeling of betrayal when a close friend can't seem to fulfill our emotional needs or make our lives work according to our personal agenda. Caretaking of our children, especially as mothers, can also supercede our ability to get in touch with the deeper dimensions of Divine Love that our Soul wishes to allow us to know.

We have all heard the announcement on the airplane that says, "Put your own mask on first before putting on the mask for those around you." This applies to all aspects of our lives. If we aren't filled with the qualities of Spirit we wish to give or receive from those around us, we are just an empty cup trying to be filled, or giving what we don't have. As we take care of filling ourselves first, others are inspired and our radiance reveals the highest choice of Divine Love for them to align with.

On a larger scale we could say our heart has every right to put its focus of attention on being safe, secure and feeling taken care of. We are pressured by world situations to live in fear that our basic needs are in jeopardy. Some of these very real concerns revolve around the threat of terrorism, the lack of provisional health care, economic instability and the sense that those in leadership positions are not taking care of our basic needs. These are very real concerns that are in the field of consciousness for all of us. It's time that we each individually come to terms with the state of fear in our hearts that we are personally perpetuating. As we recognize the fear we can ask ourselves what we are longing for that will truly allow our basic needs to feel met. We can stop believing that fear will help us in any way to meet our needs. Then it is possible to feel the natural longing that is present and ask how this longing can truly be fed so that we can each feel not only that our basic needs are being taken care of, but that we can be fed by a deeper, substantial energy of Divine Love that we trust and know is there for us. That Divine Love that fills our heart and Soul will transform our world.

The following session is an example of this transformation happening for a woman within the context of a personal relationship. Consider how freeing it would feel to live from the place that says, "All is well. You are not only taken care of, but you are held sacred. Your heart is deeply valued and your life will be ignited by that source of Divine Love radiantly moving through your heart."

From the level of your Soul and its desire for your fulfillment, this is a natural state. It is your choice: to have your heart hold the fight or flight response inherent in holding fear, or to have your heart filled with the radiance of higher Soulful Love that is connected to universal strength, stability, wisdom and support. Enjoy the following dialogue and feel your heart opening to touch higher Love.

❧

**Susann:** So, Helen, what is the theme you want to talk about today?

**Helen:** Releasing my ex-husband, Jim, so I can get on with my life. I continue to expect him to make my life work, and I don't understand why he doesn't seem to support my choices around childcare issues, and what I see.

**Susann:** We also spoke about helping you release your tendency to care take in your relationships, in favor of making space for Divine Love, which is a higher Love. When you are in the space of higher Love you naturally feel taken care of. And those you are with will also provide an authentic quality of caring for you. Often we come together in a relationship solely on the basis of wanting someone to take care of us in a way our parents didn't know how to, our childish needs are at the forefront of the relationship. Consequently, neither partner can be what the other partner is looking for because each is living from the place of the childish needs feeling unmet. Now in order to fully release this, you have to go up to a higher level that says, "I'm done with caretaking him to get love. And I am done with wanting a relationship based on a need for caretaking." Your marriage agreement, as you described it to me, was to be the nurturing mom your former husband never had, who will take care of him no matter how he treats you, physically or verbally.

**Helen:** If I loved him, that means I would take care of him because that's the only kind of love that I know, and I'm still looking to be cared for by a man, so if at least I can get that, then I am okay.

**Susann:** It seems that caretaking love comes with all sorts of pitfalls when it inappropriately appears in a situation. I understand that you are not interested in falling into these pitfalls anymore.

**Helen:** Right.

**Susann:** Would you like to name one or two of them?

**Helen:** I would, Susann! Number one: it's putting his needs before mine. This shows up in different ways. I worry about what he says and does, and how he feels, and I completely forget my own needs because I'm so busy trying to make sure that he's happy. Number two: he gets mad at me so I kind of try to dance around in my heart behind this fortress of, "I really don't love you anymore." Then I feel bad when I do that and I feel like I'm hurting him, and then he's saying, "I still love you." On some level I don't want to lose that. I still want him to love me.

**Susann:** And how would that serve you for him still to love you?

**Helen:** Well, it would make me feel like I'm fulfilling some purpose, or like I'm worthy of some kind of love. Like the more people who love me, the more I'm okay. I start putting them before me because what's more important is that they love me so I can feel lovable.

**Susann:** Thanks for your honesty. When somebody doesn't give you what you're looking for, then what happens?

**Helen:** Then I start to feel insecure, and I start obsessing about what's going on with him and how he's feeling, and where he could possibly be coming from, and how did this happen, how did it get to this place?

**Susann:** So here you are, trying to let go of someone who has been important for you as a source of love and it's very difficult to do. A tremendous fear comes with that attempt to let go, a fear you won't be taken care of if you let go of him and his love, coupled with the belief that says others, especially men, are responsible for my knowing of love. And then you are definitely up a creek without a paddle. And that's why you have that feeling of heartache, because you have given him the responsibility for your ability to feel lovable, and when he walks away, you are completely empty and pining for that person in order to know higher Love again.

**Helen:** I feel like I'm doing exactly that with my ex-husband, Jim. Am I just going to transfer that onto my current partner, Colin?

**Susann:** That is a definite possibility if you don't change the pattern. So, to be in a new relationship, you want to shift that pattern so you attract the right kind of love instead of the old pattern of more caretaking love. That pattern created the pitfalls that took you out of Divine Love, as you had anticipated, in fact. This is your time to engage your heart and Soul more deeply so you may know the kind of Divine Love you are longing for. What your heart is missing is the pure dimension of Soulful Love that truly feeds it, so it runs around looking for love in all the wrong places, as we have described.

**Helen:** Right. I have noticed with Colin that when he offers to take care of something for me I feel hurt because he does not want me to be his caretaker. I feel disappointed and not accepting of what I have to give. And then there's disappointment, or I'm a little offended.

**Susann:** It sounds like you are not comfortable allowing him to be the man who loves you from his heart and Soul, and provides for you from that level.

**Helen:** Okay.

**Susann:** What we want to do for you is help you understand what your Soul wants to give you of the true dimension of Divine Love so you can feel that for yourself and know that you can call on that source of Divine Love to feed you at any time you need to know the feeling of love. That way Divine Love is always available to you. It certainly beats the old paradigm you created that says, "I don't have it, you have it; and the only way I'm going to get it is for you to give it to me."

**Helen:** So my partner would magnify the Divine Love that I already have in myself?

**Susann:** Yes, that's what another person in our world is there for, to magnify and co-create from that shared place of Divine Love.

**Helen:** And I notice that with Colin, he compliments me constantly, and he's affectionate and he's sweet…and sometimes I don't know how to deal with it. The other night I was making dinner and he came behind me, and he was holding me and I just wanted him off of me. It was just too much.

**Susann:** Okay, so let's have you focus on that feeling. See what your heart and body are trying to say to you when you have that reaction, when Colin touches you that way.

**Helen:** It's like I can't take his affection in. There's an internal conflict.

**Susann:** You can't take it in because…?

**Helen:** Because I don't deserve it. I'm also mad at myself because I feel like there's something that can overwhelm me, and something bad will happen. I won't be able to get anything done, or it won't be what I want, or it'll go away.

**Susann:** Endless possibilities of reasons to keep love out. "I have to stay alert. I can't just take a moment to receive and drink in Divine Love, I have to keep on it, on it, on it."

**Helen:** Right! Or I'll die!

**Susann:** So it feels like there is an interesting juxtaposition inside you saying, "If I take it in, I'll die; and if I don't take it in, I'll end up being just this mere caretaker, and I will never know real love and that feels like a slow death." It's a lose-lose situation inside you.

**Helen:** I'm getting to these new levels of openness with Colin and it's really, really frightening!

**Susann:** It's scary for you to be open if your survival seems to depend on it, which is the way you have functioned in love. True openness relates to taking in more of your Soul-Essence, your divine self and who you really are. That's what true vulnerability is. To be open to receive the Divine Love that your Soul wishes to feed you.

**Helen:** That makes sense. It feels right that when he tries to give to me I just feel like I can't take it in. The old pattern is just kicking in.

**Susann:** Because you don't trust this foreign component of intimate love.

**Helen:** Right, because all that he's doing is just giving me love. I realize I don't trust it because I don't know it in myself. If I knew it inside and trusted higher Love moving in me, I would trust receiving his love. Got it.

**Susann:** So, if you were already filled with that Divine Love when he comes to hold you, it would be a time to magnify the Divine Love you know with him.

**Helen:** Yes.

**Susann:** So we are going to take a journey to your Soul, to the time when your Soul-Essence first discovered what Divine Love is. We are going to ask your Soul-Essence to bring you to that place of remembrance of what it was to be united with that. Okay?

**Helen:** Good.

*At this point Susann leads Helen in a guided meditation to journey to her Soul-Essence. To follow the meditation for yourself, go to page 229 at the end of the book.*

**Susann:** Now take that Light that's all around you beyond this space/time dimension to the field of your Soul-Essence because your Soul wishes to bring the love you are seeking to you at this time. Know as you touch into this place of Soul-Essence that the Divine Love that your body, mind and heart wish to know at this time will come in. Move into that space as if you've never left it. See what impressions, images, sensations and feelings you have.

**Helen:** Hmm, good. Feels nice. There is Light in this space, lots of it.

**Susann:** Where is the Light source coming from? What is the nature of this Light?

**Helen:** The Light seems to be everywhere and coming from different points of Spirit. It is warm. I feel physically warm and feel a sense of safety.

**Susann:** And having that presence of Light makes you feel safe in what way?

**Helen:** Protected, cared for. It's part of me.

**Susann:** And when you feel this presence, this quality of Light, do you feel cared for, as though Light is a place of pure Love for you to relax into?

**Helen:** Yes.

**Susann:** How does this Light relate to Divine Love for you?

**Helen:** It is pure Divine Love. It is the same thing. It looks like Light, but feels like Divine Love.

**Susann:** And how do you know that?

**Helen:** Because it carries qualities that allow me to feel cared for and qualities that I can trust to take in and receive.

**Susann:** When Light moves through your heart there's a feeling of Divine Love there and all those qualities you want are present.

**Helen:** That's right.

**Susann:** So Divine Love is Light moving through the heart for you. I like that. It's a divine quality. It's not an emotional love. The heart is a divine space for Light to come through. Let your heart be a holding tank for Light. See what that would be like to let your heart hold Divine Love for you.

**Helen:** It is easy to feel that and then to emanate that. I see myself walking around expressing that Light coming through my heart.

**Susann:** Wonderful. So, if you are expressing all those things, you are declaring that you are living as Divine Love. Divine Love, here I am!

**Helen:** Yes, it is beautiful, peaceful, nice.

**Susann:** How did you get this Divine Love? Did somebody give it to you? Where did it come from?

**Helen:** It's just out there, floating around, and I chose to let that essence of pure Love be a part of me.

**Susann:** So you took it in. You allowed yourself to take it in. Let's feel what it would be like to have Colin be with you while you're in this state. You could remember that moment when he came up to you and he wanted to hug you. What you told me before was that you could only take in a little bit of it and you started feeling lots of struggle. Now what does it feel like when you're filled with Divine Love in your heart to have him near?

**Helen:** Like I want to meet the love that he gives me. And give back to him and no one's sort of taking in more than the other. There is a meeting of Divine Love.

**Susann:** So, where it meets, it's not his love and your love; it's just Divine Love being amplified.

**Helen:** Right. Yeah, not like he's giving it to me but sharing it with me.

**Susann:** He's not giving it to you. You are sharing it. Very good. Now take a moment from this place and think of somebody you have done caretaking love with before. See how you look upon that previous experience from this new space of holding Light and Divine Love.

**Helen:** It looks like there's a sucking going on from that person. That person is trying to suck that Divine Love and Light from me to take it and make it his own, but he never gets filled. The Divine Love and Light just goes into a black hole. It's exhausting for me, and there's no gain for him, either. There's got to be a container around me that holds my own Light around myself and doesn't allow it to be sucked out by someone else, like I have done before.

**Susann:** That would be a choice in you that says, "I don't choose to give Divine Love away or let anyone suck it away. So you make that declaration to yourself, that you're going to protect this Divine Love and hold it sacred and you're not going to give it to anybody, not even your boyfriend. You are not giving Divine Love to that person as though you have it and he needs it. Your vow is that "I will share Divine Love but not give Divine Love away."

**Helen:** There's a part of me that wants to believe that everybody has this pure Love in them and shares it, and that it's real for people in their lives. There's a part of me that has a hard time believing that there could be somebody that is just trying to take it all the time.

**Susann:** Remember, in your previous experience with Colin, he could open the experience of amplifying Divine Love, but if you couldn't receive it, it would not be known by you. You had to learn to receive it from its source first, and then be able to magnify it with another. It's not that people don't have the pure Love in them, but they don't know how to receive it, share it, amplify it and hold it, as you found was true for you, to a certain degree.

**Helen:** So giving Divine Love to someone who doesn't know how to hold it is never going to help him. I can see how it is not valuable to give it to him because he doesn't know what to do with it.

**Susann:** Right. If they can't receive it, it will slip right through them into a black hole, as you described it.

**Helen:** Right. So my best bet is just be an example of it.

**Susann:** Exactly! Hold Divine Love and be open to share it where it exists in another. Your purpose is to hold that warm light of Divine Love and be that essence that you know you are. Feel how different it feels to hold that warm Light of Love in contrast to your previous experience as the caretaker. Before, you needed to take care of somebody so that you would feel lovable. Now you can relax and let your heart be filled with the connection to the Light of your Soul's connection to Divine Love.

**Helen:** The caretaker liked feeling uncentered and erratic. It's hard to hold onto any Light in myself when I'm so busy trying to take care of others. It makes me get off track. The relaxed, peaceful brightness of having my heart connected to the real thing is much better.

**Susann:** We always have a choice. In your case you can be that caretaker person or you can hold love. It's good to feel the difference. Then you are free to choose which way you would like to be as it relates to Divine Love.

**Helen:** Thanks.

**Susann:** What is important for you now is to keep your attention on that image of Light being everywhere. Visualize and breathe it into your heart. Then feel what it is like to have that warm Light connected to the different points of Spirit in your heart. Keep seeing that image and feel what the Light and higher Love does for you when you bring it into your heart. Then notice how you feel toward others and how that keeps clarifying and brightening and strengthening for you. Let yourself bring in this higher Love that your Soul wants you to have so your love life may be fulfilled here.

Moving to the place of higher Love that you long for begins with honesty of the heart. Put your attention on your heart as I had Helen do, and ask yourself what you want that you are not getting. You are uncovering those limitations and opening the places in yourself that have been disconnected from Divine Love, and not being fed by Divine Love. You can now reunite those empty spaces, or places of fear, with the Divine Love you truly want to have within your heart. You may now begin the journey to open to and receive the eternal nature of Divine Love that your Soul is connected to, that you are ready to receive. As you ask to receive this union with higher Divine Love, be open to the magic that wants to be known again in your heart and in life.

## Abiding With Home and Family

To know a sense of home and family seems to be as much an inherent necessity of life as breathing. Home can mean the need for basic shelter. Or it can have a deeper meaning, such as feeling at home on this planet. To know a sense of family is to feel a sense of belonging and connection. It can mean that others see and understand us and we always have a place to rest. We have those who are present to witness our life in all its colors and challenges.

Home and family are essential ingredients to the heart and Soul, and not just at the physical level. Knowing a sense of home and family truly makes our heart sing and we feel a sense of peace to our very core. Often we will do anything to acquire these components. Each of you might even be able to name what you have done to have these ingredients in your life. My Soul hungered so much for these dimensions of Soul food that I became part of a worldwide community as I describe in this book.

In retrospect, maybe we see that what we have done to create home and/or family was sometimes healthy, sometimes unhealthy. It's important for each one of us to hold the true essence of home and family so deeply and richly in our self that we can reflect and create that reality in our outer world. Home and family are a natural part of our Soul riches to be known in our very core as a foundation, as a home base for our expanded contribution while in this world.

The desire to be connected to a sense of family can draw us to all sorts of relationships. Innately, our Souls convey to us that we are part of a vast spiritual family called universal oneness. We often feel separate from that expansive womb that holds us continually and that loving presence that exists to hold all that we value to be true. In losing our sense of connection, we spend our lives attempting to re-create that satisfying state externally. I have worked with many who have had relationships with people that seem to have a hard time releasing, merely out of fear of losing that feeling of home and family they believe that relationship alone can give them. It can create a sense of loss that can feel like a space that might never be filled again. It can be unconsciously held on to for dear life. In fact, it can keep us from knowing the sense of home and family we long for, which can no longer be creatively held by that relationship or friendship.

What I have found is that each of us, in the very heart of our Soul, knows a divine connection to the spirit of family and home that our Soul was birthed from. This connection will never leave us. It has always been present for us to draw on. We have disconnected from it for a myriad of reasons, based mostly on innocence. The good news is that it is very possible to reconnect with that quality of Spirit and live here in this world in the surroundings of that pure essence of home and family that our Soul eternally carries.

The following session is an example of a client's reunion with the sacred nature of family she longs for. It also depicts her experience, which happens quite often, of having difficulty releasing her final heart ties with her former husband. In her heart and Soul he represented her opportunity to know true family, so she was reluctant to release him fully, as she unconsciously felt that meant she would be "homeless" and without family. This often happens after a death, divorce, "empty nest" or a physical move. It is so valuable to reunite with and hold the essence of family the Soul knows so we can move freely and gracefully through life filled with the inevitable nature of change along our path.

**Connie:** I want to work with releasing my connection to my ex-husband, Norman. I still want more from him than I know is appropriate. It feels like there is a heartstring in me that is not letting go. I haven't seen him for over a year, so this doesn't make sense. Maybe it is a Soul-level connection that you can help me unravel. I don't believe it's bad or anything. I just feel unnaturally tied in, and I bet it is keeping me from having another relationship show up that is truly satisfying. I don't get why I would still be hooked in. That is why I am here today.

**Susann:** Thank you for sharing your heart concerns with me, Connie. This is delicate and somewhat mysterious territory you are traversing. I understand how perplexing it must feel. On most levels Norman is out of your life completely and you are living well beyond the context of your relationship with him. The heart functions so differently than the conscious mind, especially if there is a Soul-level connection involved. The heart bonds to another person in such an intimate relationship and needs very strong guidance to train it to lessen the bond with the current heart connection. It is no small matter. The heart must be given "another choice" to bond to, to fully release its intimate bond to someone.

**Connie:** I would say that Norman, as well as his sister and other family members, gave me a sense of home and family that I had never known before. I obviously was craving it and still am.

**Susann:** That could be part of the reason you have had some difficulty releasing that connection as fully as you want to. At a Soul level, why would you want to lose connection to home and family? Norman and his family held that for you.

**Connie:** Yes! I really want to create a real family for myself now. It has felt like something has held me back from taking steps in that direction. Wow. That's true. I see how it all fits. Okay. I'm ready to release that whole ball of wax and get on with my life. I'm glad we can do this.

**Susann:** It feels like what we want to do today is to reconnect you to your original umbilical cord of connection to the essence of home and family that your Soul has always known. In fact, your Soul has always been held by that connection. Somehow we seem to lose track of this connection in this world, so we spend our lifetime trying to re-create it in numerous shapes and forms.

**Connie:** That makes sense. But will I lose connection to the rest of his family now?

**Susann:** Oh, gosh no. What is valuable and true to you will remain. It will not be a need, but a desire for you. More freeing, for sure. As you make this shift you won't have to hold that thread of connection to

Norman to keep that essence intact. It's not appropriate, as you recognize. It's not his job to hold that for you. The good news is that when you re-create it *within* yourself you can attract the home and family situation in the outer world that truly serves you and nourishes your heart, Soul and body.

**Connie:** That would be great.

**Susann:** Okay. Let's open the door for you to have the experience you came for.

*At this point Susann leads Connie in a guided meditation to journey to her Soul-Essence. To follow the meditation for yourself, go to page 229 at the end of the book.*

**Susann:** As you bring "all that you are," surrounded by illuminating Light, may this Light take you to the place in your Soul-Essence that carries pure, eternal connection to the Spirit of home and family. Let "all that you are" open to receive and reunite with this Spirit of home and family. Let the Light guide you to the space where this exists within you, as though it never left you. Feel yourself touching that field with all that you are. What's that like for you in that space?

**Connie:** Peaceful. People are all around a table. People playing games. They are being together in a joyful way. Everyone has something to offer. It's filling my entire house.

**Susann:** You mean the one you are currently living in?

**Connie:** Yes.

**Susann:** It sounds like you are filling your house with the spirit of home. How does your body feel?

**Connie:** Relaxed. Full. I feel playful. That feels important. Supportive.

**Susann:** How do you know that this isn't just your imagination or a fairy tale you are making up?

**Connie:** Because I can feel it. It's not just a picture in my mind. I remember when I first met Norman I didn't feel what people describe as romantic love. Norman felt like home to me. So this is nice to feel without having to have Norman around. I like this.

**Susann:** This home space carries a feeling that your heart and Soul can rest in. They can rest in something larger.

**Connie:** Yes.

**Susann:** This space holds you, and all that you are, sacred. The playfulness you are mentioning signifies that you can be alive, playful and joyful when the essence of home for you is present.

**Connie:** I like it here.

**Susann:** So now I would like you to take a moment to make a declaration, internally or externally, that you are saying, with every fiber of your being and every cell of your body: "This is what I want to know and experience here in this life and in my body."

**Connie:** I am home. I am happy. I have a joyful partner and an extended family that are joyful, peaceful, playful, beautiful and nurturing.

**Susann:** Take a moment and breathe all this in.

**Connie:** Wow! I feel the energy of a man nearby that just popped in and feels very real.

**Susann:** Ask that energy to come closer.

**Connie:** I see. This male energy, this man feels at home in my home.

**Susann:** Anything else showing up?

**Connie:** Yes, an energy of sister or niece. Something like that.

**Susann:** This feels like an essence of family that is important to you.

**Connie:** Yes. That has always been important to me. I really want that in my life as part of family for me.

**Susann:** You can now draw on these Soul connections you have seen with you to help you provide a true sense of home and family here in this world. It does not have to be just a feeling you create during a meditation such as this. You are connecting to what it takes to truly have that essence as a real-life experience.

**Connie:** I'm ready to make this happen.

**Susann:** Great. Your job, your "homework," is to keep in your heart these pictures and feelings that came to you today. Give yourself permission to be surrounded by this wealth of home and family. Let it bathe you, nurture you and bring you the relaxed, joyful satisfaction you've known today.

**Connie:** Sounds like a wonderful assignment to me.

**Susann:** May this spirit of family that you know now bring great richness to your life.

**Connie:** I'm excited.

# Knowing True Relationship With Love

In the field of searching for the right relationship, it is so essential to begin that right relationship within us. Our true relationship with Divine Love is foundational to our ability to know how to have the kind of love relationships that truly satisfy us, heart and Soul. This includes not just intimate partnership, but how we interact with all those around us, whether it is in family, business or friendship. To be in love successfully begins with the ability to know what Divine Love feels like within one's own heart and body, so we approach others with our cup at least half full. It's much better to be full, rather than empty and lonely, looking for love in the wrong places because we attract other empty people. Our Soul is deeply committed to our knowing of connection to the heart of Divine Love that we may live life radiantly in love with the joy of creating.

The following session can assist in reuniting you with your true relationship to Divine Love.

**Susann:** What would you like to focus on today, Leslie?

**Leslie:** What's happening is that I'm looking to start a new life, but I feel like I've had blinders on up until this point, so I don't exactly know what direction to take. My background is nursing. I've been in hospitals for about 30 years, but I haven't had my heart in it for a while. So I know that the timer is on and I'll be out of there pretty soon. Or maybe it's I just won't be there that often.

**Susann:** How has nursing and what you've done in the hospitals served you?

**Leslie:** I have compassion for people in pain. I also think I don't like being alone, so I keep going to the hospital to avoid being alone. I'm willing to give and serve and everything, but I now feel I need to be fed too.

**Susann:** Right. You deserve it.

**Leslie:** So here I am. I also want to see how all this relates to being alone and not being in a significant relationship. I feel even more alone when I have been working at the hospital. You would think it would be the opposite, but it's not. And I find myself attracted to the wrong kind of men to fill that emptiness I feel when I am outside of work.

**Susann:** As I see it, when you are at work you are putting out that wonderful love that is such a special part of your Soul makeup because you feel that others really need it. They deserve to have it, so you will give it to them. That seems natural. But, in fact, you are giving your very essence of Divine Love away, so you feel empty and lonely the more you are around others. When you are this generous with men who are hungry for love, you probably feel taken advantage of and don't understand why you don't get much back from them. The fact is you have poured out your heart to them, before they even ask for it, because you feel if you give it to them they will return it to you. You give. You empty yourself. They can't receive it all. And, when it doesn't come back in return, you end up feeling even more empty.

**Leslie:** Yes. I'm isolated because of those kinds of guys I find myself attracted to.

**Susann:** We want to help you remember what it is like to hold the essence of Love that you are within yourself, so that it feeds you and fills you. Then you are a beacon of Divine Love, not a package of love just to be given away to the first taker. When you are a beacon of Divine Love, you attract men who value and cherish that and hold it sacred. You must do this in yourself first. Then your very presence in the hospital uplifts you and you don't have to be so drained and emptied by your work.

**Leslie:** Okay, I'm ready. My heart is so happy!

**Susann:** Okay, so we're going to take a journey today to help reestablish, at a Soul level, your connection to Divine Love.

*At this point Susann leads Leslie in a guided meditation to journey to her Soul-Essence. To follow the meditation for yourself, go to page 229 at the end of the book.*

**Susann:** Let the Light that surrounds you take you to the place of remembrance in your Soul of your exquisite and pure connection to Divine Love. Let yourself receive that pure Love as your divine birthright.

**Leslie:** I've been so alone here in this Earth world. In the space my Soul has taken me to I am recognizing home again and the pure Love is definitely overwhelming. I have felt such a huge pain without this. The pain of not being recognized for who I am. The pain of carrying everybody's pain, from my family to, oh, my God, there's years of people's pain from the hospital where I work. Somehow I thought that my greatest gift was compassion, and that to really understand compassion, you need to understand pain. So I got caught in others' pain to have compassion for them. Well, maybe that's a misunderstanding that I've been told all along.

**Susann:** I feel like you are very ready to let go of knowing compassion as the highest form of love you give yourself permission to know. You have felt that compassion was the only kind of love known here. What you are really expressing is sympathy for others' pain. You are hoping that if you resolve their pain, they will be free to love and you will have people to love you and you won't feel so alone. Many do this.

**Leslie:** Yes, yes. I see that. I *do* want that feeling of pure Love I feel right now as I touch that space of home I am part of. I see the blue stars. They're all around me. I just went through a huge shift talking about my tendency to be compassionate. I know now I am just sympathetic to others' pain. I am getting that pain out of my heart now. I see that I've chosen to be in that realm of sympathy to get love and now I don't need to be there anymore. Basically, I've felt like I've been a healing garbage pail for everybody's pain and emotion so that's what got me into spiritual work to begin with, to try to learn how to move that energy out. So now I just feel there's a different quality of growth that's possible without taking care of others all the time.

**Susann:** Yes, you can now feel this connection to Divine Love as your true world. You can be of that world. Here in this world you are "in this world" but not "of it", because your heart is already given to your true world of Divine Love, which means everything to you, as it should.

**Leslie:** It's as you said, being in the world but not of it. Now I have an electrical cord that I see coming from that home filled with blue stars. I can plug into my heart on a daily basis to remember where I'm from, and what pure Love is for me. I can have a relationship with pure Love myself.

**Susann:** Yes, it's your time to remember that you came from Divine Love and that you know that in your Soul. Your song is: "I already know of the depth and breadth of this Divine Love that makes my heart sing with my truth."

**Leslie:** I can see now, with the information I'm getting, that I'm being supported in a different way to hold that space of pure Love. The blue stars represent that for me.

**Susann:** Tell me more about the nature and quality of this support you now feel.

**Leslie:** That, with this shift, I have a different support system that keeps me in this realm of Divine Love that I can call on anytime.

**Susann:** You know you have a real support system that "gets" you.

**Leslie:** Yes! And also with this shift I have just had, I see that I tried to help others out of their pain because I didn't know how to get myself out of my own pain. It's like I could have a vicarious experience of being out of pain through having compassion for them that might hopefully shift my world. The difference is that I was in pain, so I saw pain, and so that is gone and now I'm remembering the depth of that pure Love and my world becomes pure Love. Wow, I can actually rest in something.

**Susann:** Exactly.

**Leslie:** I literally see the different shifts in the old world that I lived in and the new world that is now my world. It's much lighter in my heart! I don't have that deep, pulling pain kind of feeling. It feels lighter; I never thought it could be different. I feel it in my belly too.

**Susann:** I'm so happy for you and your heart and body!

**Leslie:** So is my old imprint of being afraid I'll be taken advantage of gone? Can I stop attracting unavailable men too?

**Susann:** Yes, we're replacing these patterns with something that you value more. You are saying, in essence, "I choose to create from this new place now. I choose to hold this frequency in my heart."

Now, what I want you to do, just to confirm that, is to imagine somebody that you know, or simply feel an energy that wishes to take advantage of you, while you're in this Light place. Just have it show up and see how you feel about it now.

**Leslie:** When I do that it looks like there's a bubble around me, which that person is unable to permeate so that they are just on the periphery. They can't get within a five-foot radius. They are unable to get into that realm that I hold.

**Susann:** Is it a protective bubble?

**Leslie:** Let's see. It's actually a bubble holding the pure Love. They can't get in because they don't know how to hold pure Love. So, with that bubble in place, as I now live in this world, does this Love energy start moving out even more? Does it get bigger? Is that something that I have control over?

**Susann:** I feel like you're going to answer your own question as you live from this new space in yourself. It will expand and contract where the need is. If you're talking about needing to love a child or an intimate partner, it will create depth and there will be merging, communion and connection within it. If it just relates to being able to help a patient, it won't expand. It will just be available for you to hold Divine Love radiantly within yourself so you don't revert back to your sympathetic self. You are absolutely in charge of it. And you are supported by the field of Divine Love that you touched in your home with the blue stars in it.

**Leslie:** I can feel it in my cells. I can feel Divine Love. Definitely my hands feel like electricity is moving through them.

**Susann:** That is so wonderful. Now let's see what happens when I suggest to you that you might be physically alone.

**Leslie:** That is no longer an issue. I feel like there are different beings around me as a reminder that if it gets intense, they are a reminder for me to remember to plug in. And, also, the communication has shifted. There's an understanding that they're communicating through my knowingness. It seems like it has really shifted. I'm not questioning, "Well, am I making this up?" It's a known.

**Susann:** Excellent.

**Leslie:** I've wanted this for a long time, so I see that shift. But I see now that whatever the old world was before, it's now moving out. I can see it moving to my right farther and farther away. That's very reassuring.

**Susann:** Yes, you're doing great.

**Leslie:** You know this is a really different feeling. It's almost like the air is different. It's lighter. And there's an energy coming out my hands that I could heal with. There's a level of love that's coming through and can transform. I've wanted that for a long time.

**Susann:** Yes, you are a real conduit for this Divine Love now. That's much better than giving it away, which leaves you empty and sends out the message that people can take advantage of this empty feeling while they are looking for love.

**Leslie:** Like there are different waves coming in. It's very peaceful. I want to stay here.

**Susann:** You may hold this place in yourself forever. And, if you stray away temporarily, just see the blue stars and feel that Divine Love field as a bubble around you and you will draw it right back in. Your Soul and heart and cells are now lined up to do this as naturally as breathing.

**Leslie:** I feel very in love. Thank you for this magical time.

Leslie called me a week later to say she had "just happened" to meet a very special man. She wasn't looking for him at all. He literally walked into her life. She was so happy to say that she knew she was holding this pure connection to Divine Love in her heart, which she knew was her natural gift, and she could be truly seen now, in the deepest way possible.

## Singing Your Heart Song

How often have we felt like giving up on this thing called love. Our heart and Soul know that it is what we are here to experience in all its facets and colors, but the minute we open up to know and enjoy our hearts' longing, old fears come up that try to make us believe we should shut down the magic because it will only hurt us in the end.

Fear does such an excellent job of stopping our life's dance. The fact is that when the heart is filled with fear we are disconnected from Divine Love and we will feel the results or effects of that disconnection. The disconnect shows itself through such primary ways as feeling unloved, unwanted, abandoned and helpless. In this state we imagine that our heart is being hurt.

It is our disconnection to Divine Love that is the nature of the pain being felt. To attempt to assuage our fear of feeling our heart hurt we try to protect our heart. This attempt to protect what we value can backfire on us. We start relying on the protection around our heart to keep us safe, secure and free from harm. We depend on it so thoroughly that its very existence within us crystallizes, hardens and creates a wall. This wall not only keeps the perceived dangers out, but also keeps out the connection, the love, the joy and the ability to co-create.

Mother Teresa states it beautifully: "The biggest disease today is not leprosy or tuberculosis, but rather the feeling of being unwanted, uncared for and deserted by everybody."

Our protective wall keeps us from feeling loved, wanted and trusting others to love us. It is paramount for all of us to reunite with our heart and Soul's connection to Divine Love that allows us to connect deeply with others. Divine Love is the pure food that feeds us and allows us to know the love we are truly longing for. Then we have a barometer within us that knows what true love feels like that we can trust. Then we can trust our heart to know when and how to share its radiance and wealth. Without this connection we can feel unsafe to open our heart and unsure of who and what to let in. Only our connection to Divine Love is real and sacred and can fill our heart space. Others might come and go, according to their Soul's movement and choices, but our heart remains filled with connection to pure Love.

The following is an example of what that process looks and feels like and how special it is to know Divine Love as the true space of home the heart can rest in.

**Claudia:** I want so badly to feel like I am free to love another human being. I get close to a man and I can feel all those barbs coming up in front of my heart, shouting, "No! No! Don't trust him. Don't go there." And on the other hand, of course, the deeper part of my heart says everything is about Divine Love and it's all okay and Divine Love is what you are. It's such a little battle that goes on inside me. It makes me feel crazy, and then I feel like such a loser that I think maybe I should just cut off this relationship thing until I grow up. That's a joke. I'm already 45. So you see my dilemma.

**Susann:** I certainly feel for you. I witness this pattern with men and women all the time. So let's see what we can do to give you what your Soul is truly longing for so that your heart can feel filled to over-flowing with the nectar of the gods, so to speak. Then you will be free to co-create here with the beautiful people in your life who wish to share the riches of love with you in a myriad of ways. You are such a natural at love. We don't want that to go to waste just because of a silly little block trying to sabotage you.

**Claudia:** Absolutely. I feel like a racehorse waiting for the race to begin.

**Susann:** Let's get going then, and focus our attention on bringing the gifts of your Soul forward so you may remember the Divine Love you are made of.

*At this point Susann leads Claudia in a guided meditation to journey to her Soul-Essence. To follow the meditation for yourself, go to page 229 at the end of the book.*

**Susann:** Let that brilliant Light that shines all around you take you to the essence of your Soul, which knows what it is to abide in the eternal nature of Divine Love. Let yourself bring forth the Light that you are, to connect and commune with that place your heart and Soul knows deep inside. Let yourself merge with that essence, and when you are ready to share your experience, please feel free to speak.

**Claudia:** I see a path to a garden, like a paradise garden.

**Susann:** Sense how this garden feels to you.

**Claudia:** I want to cry. It's so gorgeous and I'm all by myself.

**Susann:** Shall we call others to be with you in the garden of your heart?

**Claudia:** Yeah. I see other beings showing up like Light bubbles. It feels like I'm invisible.

**Susann:** Okay, so they are there, but you're not connecting.

**Claudia:** Yeah, they're just sort of hovering around. I'm afraid I'm repelling them, like a positive versus a negative. It feels like I am nonexistent.

**Susann:** Let's go inside you and find out what puts you into the negative and nonexistent space. What are you feeling? What's going on inside?

**Claudia:** Longing.

**Susann:** You feel a longing, and yet there is something holding your heart back or there wouldn't just be a longing. Do you see what I mean?

**Claudia:** That's right. I see this teeny little black stone, in a square. It's very small, but it must have quite a bit of density to it, like a black hole or something.

**Susann:** Tell me more.

**Claudia:** It's coming into my field, circling around, not really in my body. It's doing something.

**Susann:** How is it influencing you? How do you feel about having it there?

**Claudia:** I don't like it, but it's there.

**Susann:** Okay, does it feel like the longing happens and then the black hole comes in? How does it feel that the black hole influences the longing?

**Claudia:** I don't know, but it's disrupting my field.

**Susann:** So it's keeping your heart from fulfilling its longing for true divine connection.

**Claudia:** Somehow, but I don't know how it's doing that.

**Susann:** Can you ask the black hole what it wants from you and your heart?

**Claudia:** Wow. It says it is there to protect me. How strange. How can something disruptive protect me? It doesn't make sense.

**Susann:** Go back to the gorgeous garden. See if it is there with you.

**Claudia:** It is around me as I go down the path. Oh, I get it. When it is around, it keeps me invisible. Oh. It's protecting me and keeping me from the other Lights I want to be with in the garden.

**Susann:** Return to the moment on the path that you said okay to the black hole, that it was okay for it to protect you.

**Claudia:** I was a bright and shining Light coming out of the garden to take my Soul exploring. Somehow this black thing came in and I got confused.

**Susann:** So you let it stick around because you didn't understand it.

**Claudia:** Yeah. I figured it had a good reason for being there. So it tagged along and then when I went back home, to my gorgeous garden, it had gotten bigger and was now around me. So I was invisible to my Light buddies, the bubbles.

**Susann:** How are you feeling about that?

**Claudia:** I don't want it this way anymore. I don't want the black hole around. What can I do about this? It doesn't want to go away.

**Susann:** Do you need some help?

**Claudia:** Definitely.

**Susann:** Okay. So feel again how wonderful you feel inside yourself in the gorgeous garden. Never mind the black hole outside you right now.

**Claudia:** Oh, that feels good. My heart could weep again. It feels so special.

**Susann:** So use the amazing power of that connection that lives within your heart and Soul to hire a "gardener being." He is present now to hold precious and sacred what is in the garden around you and the garden of Divine Love in your heart.

**Claudia:** Oh, he's lovely. He's a moving statue of Light that comes into the garden and is so bright the black hole virtually gets jet-propelled out by the force of pure Light.

**Susann:** That's right. Divine Love overpowers anything in its presence. And Divine Love certainly does not need protection. Its radiance dispels anything less.

**Claudia:** The Light bubbles have now made circles all around me and are creating a vibration with their voices. They are talking in a vibration that is quite pure. That is so fun.

**Susann:** Can you take that pure vibration in? Feel what happens next when you are able to take that pure vibration in.

**Claudia:** Things have changed. I can feel the vibration. I just started dancing. And then I started dancing with them like we are in a Maypole dance.

**Susann:** Okay, describe the nature of your connections now.

**Claudia:** They've made me know that Divine Love is really light in the sense that it's not heavy. They're saying that it's always been in my heart. And now the energy, that black hole that was there before, I can see it but I'm not holding on to it. I feel that black hole is lessening. If I just practice letting it go, then I can feel the lightness back in my heart. The lightness has colors to it. I now feel filled with the Light of the dance. We're all playing. But I don't understand how I could have let all this beauty stop being in me.

**Susann:** You haven't been fully able to play because this black hole was in the way. It made you feel as though you were tainted and no one would want to play with you. So you had to find others who were tainted with connections to black holes to play with instead of the light-hearted buddies your heart naturally used to feel connected to. You are changing how you relate to others and whom you want to relate to. You want to play and connect. You don't want to be protected. You want to go with what you know deeply. You can now hold this energy you just created and meditate with it; as you allow it to be real in you every day, it starts to build a magnet in you and you can say, "This is who I am. I don't have this pain anymore. This is pure energy that I am and I want to magnetize to me those who are available to use this energy."

**Claudia:** And we play together. That is the nature of relationships for me now.

**Susann:** Feel where you now are and compare it to how you felt before with that black hole present. You had an invisible something around you that kept you from really being connected. That's why you would attract people who couldn't go to that place of deeply connecting. You were attracting those who had the weakness that you had. They also have had something like your black hole in their heart, disrupting them from connecting to love. You both carried this false protection.

We spoke earlier of men who have been attracted to you. It felt to you as though these men did not allow you to go to that place of deep connection that your heart longed to experience. Now you recognize that it was this place you had created in your heart for this black hole that kept you from connecting. This black hole was supposed to protect your heart, but it only disrupted it. These men were a direct reflection of what was going on in your heart. They came to protect, but they disrupted your connection to pure Love. Can you see how this pattern is the same?

**Claudia:** Yeah.

**Susann:** Now I invite you to feel that natural longing for connection and communion in Divine Love, and let yourself focus on the experience of being in your garden of Divine Love and joy with the gardener present that holds your joy-filled garden sacred. Feel what it is like to then bring others, who also hold Divine Love and joy as sacred, into your sacred garden. They are the only ones allowed in.

**Claudia:** It's like passionate play. It certainly has a lot of energy flowing, like a power network.

**Susann:** Right. Good.

**Claudia:** You know I feel like all of my life I wanted to be in that beautiful place but I couldn't. Then I'd go into a real collapse. It really is like the story of my life. I so often feel alone in a beautiful place.

**Susann:** And now you have experienced what it is to feel connected and fully supported in your heart, and to be reminded that you can always carry that in your heart.

**Claudia:** Yeah. I have always known that. At the same time it was so weird that that little, teeny black hole was present and it was orbiting in my field, and it was having such a binding influence on my heart and life. Wow!

**Susann:** Isn't that amazing?

**Claudia:** That is so bizarre. I could not have made that up.

**Susann:** That's right. It may seem like a funny little picture that makes no sense to your linear brain, but your heart and Soul helped you create that picture to heal the pattern of feeling alone, separate and unsupported. Spirit certainly works in magical ways. I see this over and over again. And here you are, having a whole new perspective on your life. We're listening to your Soul's voice speaking through your subconscious and conscious mind and heart.

**Claudia:** I loved how those Light beings just sang in such a high vibration that the teeny black hole had to pop out. That was amazing.

**Susann:** Your experience is symbolic of the true healing, transforming process. We think we have to get rid of our issues by working through them, or undoing all the layers of emotion and trauma. I find it is so much easier, quicker and even pain-free to go to a higher place in our Soul to dissolve what doesn't vibrate with us anymore.

**Claudia:** Exactly. It no longer fits. That's exactly how those Light beings with me did it. They never touched it, never really focused on it. It's so interesting, what happened the moment that I got centered in my garden. It was like the moment that I asked for help, they were right there, kind of curious almost. And then they didn't put any attention on this tiny black hole, but they were aware of it. And this is how they changed it, through a circle of sound. Then after it popped out, they kept singing to heal the opening in the field where it popped out.

**Susann:** Yes, absolutely.

**Claudia:** It felt a lot more truthful to have it happen that way. It was peaceful. I feel connected to this beautiful peaceful sense of existence now.

**Susann:** That's fabulous. Now it is your privilege to hold what you just created as sacred and deeply valuable to you to remind your Soul, your heart and all your cells that this is the beautiful inner place you now come from. You can visualize that beautiful energy of Light-filled Love and support, especially when you are feeling the natural longing for Divine Love and connection. Now you can allow yourself to have it anytime. It's just a breath away.

**Claudia:** It certainly awakens in me the remembrance that I am here for ecstatic bliss or ecstatic love. It feels so good to know how natural it is for me to know that experience again.

**Susann:** That's so wonderful. Your Soul has always known that this is true for you. Your Soul has always held that remembrance for you in the Soul DNA. Consider the fact that you had a longing to know ecstatic bliss. How would you have longed for it if you didn't know it was a reality, a possibility, a state of existence that you know of at some level? Think of it as a dimension of yourself that you got disconnected from, or which simply got covered up. We can't speak a word that we haven't heard or don't have in our vocabulary. In the field of sound and healing, it has been discovered that we can only give voice to the sounds we can hear. If we retrain the way we hear, the result, in simple terms, is a refurnishing of the brain with the missing frequencies. These frequency deficiencies are often the root cause of many life-robbing afflictions.

In the same way, at the level of the Soul we can't experience something we haven't first "heard" in our Soul. You just had the experience of hearing your Soul's song and that is ecstatic bliss. That is what you have longed for but felt was only possible through certain types of interactions. Now you are free to know the bliss you longed for within yourself by focusing your heart and mind at any time you choose on this sacred, rich song of your Soul you have reawakened.

**Claudia:**  I am very happy to be back home. Thank you.

# Longing for Sacred Union

Deep within the core of our being is a natural longing to know sacred union with the Divine. Our sexuality is a way to give that union expression. Understanding that is the first step. Experiencing that is the second. The Soul knows how to walk us through the mistranslation of our sexual urges so that we can commune again with the beauty of our sexuality and bring it to our experience of full radiance and pleasure. Our sexuality is designed to be a potent tool for creative manifestation. Sexual intimacy affords the opportunity to heighten and expand what is longing to come into fruition through us. What if we approached our sexuality with our heart and Soul already filled with sacred union with the Divine? How would this change the way we use the power of sexuality in our lives? When our Soul is engaged, we manifest a Soulful affair of sacred reunion with the Divine through the jewel of sexuality.

**Zachary:** Today I would like to speak about my sexuality. I seem to be confused as to what I want from sex. Sex is really important for me to experience in relationship to my spirituality. I have so many parts and voices speaking that I feel dissatisfied and never really present. I have taken many classes on sacred sexuality, and I still have not grasped how to align with my spirit around the topic of sex and sexual attraction.

**Susann:** Thank you for your honesty, Zachary. I want you to remember that behind every issue is a truth that your Soul wishes to open to you. I believe that you are here today because your Soul is peeking through your heart, wanting to share with you the place of deeper connection and meaning you are wishing to know and to plug into your daily life. Would you say this is true?

**Zachary:** That sounds right. That resonates. I think you can help me get there. Let me describe some of the patterns that trip me up. I have one voice that comes in when I'm in connection and intimate with my girlfriend. It's the voice that says that there's someone better, the grass is greener. Am I cheating myself; is there something more? Actually, this is happening whether I'm in an intimate relationship in any given moment or not. I'm constantly looking. I have a mind that is constantly looking for a sexy girl, just like a teenage boy. I'm constantly looking for a true love, a Soulmate, and I look at everybody through that lens. My father is a photographer. His hobby is taking pictures of women. When he used to tell my brothers and me about it, when we were young men, we just cringed. Something about it was perverted.

And my eldest brother is the biggest womanizer. And he's had three or four women a night. I had some friends who told me he was sick because he never goes home without a girl, no matter what. When I was 21 and at a bar with my brother, he'd be with this girl, and then he'd be gone. He'd take her somewhere, have sex with her and then come back. That's the background. So I decided when I was young that I was going to be spiritual. I didn't want anything to do with that stuff. I didn't want to hurt anyone. I wasn't going to do this.

I'm constantly looking at women sexually, thinking, wishing, dreaming, hoping but never really going there or acting on it. So obviously this is like a disease that I want to get rid of. I've been honest with my girlfriend. I don't really know if I could be married because I have this thing that I've never really played out. I don't know what it is. I said, "Can you imagine the books I could've written, the paintings I could've painted, the life I could've lived, how I could've really been present with people, how I could've been married long ago and really happy if I wasn't always looking?" That energy constantly ruins my day.

And it used to be even worse. I used to follow people. I could be having a good day, clearing my head and going about my business, but then there's some girl in the room. Other times I would actually swing the car back around to take a second look at someone. I'm so conscious of it now. I say to myself, "What are you really doing? It never leads to anything, you never act on it. All it's going to do is rev up your feeling of what you don't have. You're being deprived. You can't follow through.

You're not a man." It's time for me to put this on the table and have somebody help me with this.

**Susann:** So you want to see how this pattern is pertinent to you at the level of the Soul. We want to be with your Soul-Essence and see what it has to say about this behavior and the truth in back of it for you. I believe, and I have seen this over and over again, that behind every distorted behavior is a true longing to have an experience that is a valuable part of your Soul and what it wants to know in this human existence. Remember, Zachary, one of the primary reasons your particular Soul came here was to have the infinite experiences there are to be known in this amazing world of spiritual beings consciously experiencing creation through the physical capacity. Sexuality is one aspect of creation for the purpose of knowing sacred union with the Divine, the beloved All That Is.

Sacred union with the Divine is at the heart of all nature. Nature inherently expresses this union to remind us what is possible in life. When you are in nature, you have the opportunity to sense that frequency. For you, that's simply a turn-on, so to speak. Your attraction to women is, at a heart and Soul level, a longing to know the experience of sacred union here, in your physical capacity, which your Soul-Essence knows well. So every time you see a woman your cells come alive with the potential to know this sacred union also.

I can help you learn how to feel that sense of being in sacred union with the Divine. Your male and female energy may then merge within you as a spiritual experience that you create for yourself. You may then magnify that sense of sacred union within your self and your cells so that the longing is fulfilled. You'll find you can radiantly bring that home to further create with your girlfriend, or use it to go out and magnify what you love to create or produce in the world.

**Zachary:** That's what I'm after. I want to erase the patterning and triggering of my brother and my father and all their stuff, and the world I grew up in, and know a real experience around sex that rings true for me, like you are describing.

**Susann:** The feeling of being in sacred union with the Divine resonates in a more expanded and free way. When you say yes to that way, it takes the place of the old patterns you want to release. It will replace the old patterns with the resource you now value more.

**Zachary:** But I get the idea that even if you're able to do that now it's only momentary. It's asking a little too much to just replace the old patterns, because these little triggers at the neuron level or brain level are so patterned after 50 years. "Look at that woman when you're driving." It's disempowering to me at this point. It's like being possessed by something that's not me, not my Soul, not my spirit. I've always known it, and I even made a decision to be celibate in my twenties to deal with it. In the last ten years I'm more conscious of it, but it's still happening. A few years ago, I became conscious of it and started reading books on Tantra, and taking some seminars and classes to help me be present. But then I didn't really carry it out. Maybe for the first 15 minutes of sex I'm in a very conscious kind of place and then I fall more to the animal side.

**Susann:** Your mind does not believe it's possible to make that kind of overnight change, but your heart and Soul know it's very easy to make the shift.

**Zachary:** The other pattern I work with is my incessant questioning in myself. Is my girlfriend really the one? In the future, is she really going to be the one, because maybe there's somebody else? And then I remember, "Be in the present." I'm okay when I'm speaking from my heart, and I tell myself at the end of the day, "Hey! When you're in your heart and you're just being here, you feel good with her."

**Susann:** You are discovering that when you are in your heart and connected to your Soul you feel true to your divine self.

**Zachary:** When I was driving over here today I was thinking of that. She's the one today to share my divine experience with. That's all that matters.

**Susann:** She is the reflection of this sacred union place that you want to live from. She reflects that for you right now.

**Zachary:** And she has a choice to be there, or not.

**Susann:** Right.

**Zachary:** I'm fully present, I'm fully aware, and I have a choice to be here or not. And, when I'm fully present, right now, it's feeling good. And, yeah, one of us may decide a week from now, a year from now, a day from now, at the end of a lifetime, three lifetimes from now, that this is not right, and it will just come when it comes, but right now, today, I live in that house with her, and we have this beautiful child. When I'm fully present, I know the most loving, intimate, real experience of communication, verbally and physically, that I've ever had! It's good. End of story.

**Susann:** Exactly. At the same time, there is a piece of truth to these funky little sayings that show up, like "the grass is always greener." It's true. I could be in a deeper, higher, richer, greener place. When you go into the place that says, "I'm constantly looking for something better," ask yourself, "What am I really saying? I'm looking for something better within myself. It's a richer, deeper experience within myself that I'm looking for."

**Zachary:** So, rather than stopping in the place of feeling ashamed for what I think I lack, or for looking at every girl that goes by, or thinking I could have a better experience on another piece of turf, it's to recognize that I want a more authentic place of connection and union with my Soul and divine nature. There is nothing wrong with not being satisfied or feeling unfulfilled.

**Susann:** Exactly! It is a time to ask what your Soul wants to give you that you have been cut off from experiencing. So today we are going to do just that. We are going to reunite you with the experience of sacred union to the Divine at a Soul level and bring that into your heart and body and living experience. Keep your attention on your heart and your desire to know what your Soul wants to share with you.

*At this point Susann leads Zachary in a guided meditation to journey to his Soul-Essence. To follow the meditation for yourself, go to page 229 at the end of the book.*

**Susann:** Allow yourself to move into that space we're calling sacred union that your Soul knows so well. Describe a little bit about that experience when you are ready.

**Zachary:** You know what I just saw? Crystalline flowers spraying into the sky. And I'm breathing through my heart.

**Susann:** Bring that crystalline flower into your heart. And now bring that crystalline flower into your whole body. Feel it in your arms, legs and down to your toes. Feel what it feels like to exist as that crystalline flower. And feel what you are connected to universally. See how you would describe that. What's it like to exist as the crystalline flower, and be connected, in union, with the universal component that guides you?

**Zachary:** I just feel like I'm a thousand stars sparkling like diamonds and the field spreads out from me; but there is some kind of cohesive energy that I'm focused on at the same time; but I just kind of see it as a face or eyes, and loving focus in that moment, that field of sparkling Light.

**Susann:** Excellent description. So you're everything and you're an aspect of that everything all at the same time.

**Zachary:** Yes, I'm a focus point. I'm a beautiful male energy base but I'm also a flower.

**Susann:** So, from that place, what I want you to sense is what it would be like when you're in that crystalline flower emerging from the male energy base, connected to a thousand stars sparkling like diamonds, and you put your attention in front of you on your family of origin. How do you view them and their behavior? How do they show up?

**Zachary:** I see them from this state of compassion, like little "jokers" doing little tricks around me, trying to bite my toes. They are cute little tricksters.

**Susann:** Laughable and lighthearted.

**Zachary:** Right. They have little jester costumes and they're getting away with doing something. I don't care. I just laugh at their antics.

**Susann:** Now I want you to feel what it is like to see random women in the street. Feel what happens for you.

**Zachary:** I feel beautiful as I observe, precious and present. I am like a focal point, observing whatever else appears in my field. I love to breathe in their beauty and it's gorgeous! They don't appear as objects for me to take from or possess. They show up as graceful lines and beautiful shapes, beautiful coloring. It's just so beautiful!

**Susann:** Can you feel how their appearance in your field is something to experience as part of the field in your focal point? It's all just a part of this field. You never leave your field of connection to everything true. You never leave this place of male energy base connected to the crystalline flower that is part of the thousand stars.

**Zachary:** It's beautiful. It's gorgeous! Each is another star sparkling. I'm like those pictures of the great Buddha, God of the universe, sitting as He views the Earth, watching. That's how it feels. I'm breathing with it. It feels like I am breathing it.

**Susann:** I sense that you are breathing it and creating it in the moment, at the same time. This beauty is the crystalline flower your focal point created. It's not this thing out there that you want to take in and have and possess. It is an aspect of being. You are admiring an aspect of creation that is in your space.

**Zachary:** I see it now. That's what it is from this perspective.

**Susann:** This experience is the same experience you have if you are out in nature. You are admiring every aspect of the beauty of creation.

**Zachary:** It's like finding a flower that I want to bring home to my daughter and I can't pick one. I just can't pick and kill that flower. I'm trying to find one, and to do that is just starting to get old. It's so beautiful that I don't want to pick it. I just want it to be. I'm a picture taker. But not with a camera. Just by being there. I don't want to "catch" her, like my father, and own it and control it. I don't want to be on that trip. I can do it in this moment and I can do this in my life now. I see the true perspective of what my Soul wanted to experience. I just added the distortion I learned when I was growing up. Now I want to delete the distortion. I want to go back to having the pure experience with the beauty all around me. That is having sacred union with the beauty of life, like you said.

**Susann:** Great. Experience that. Bring it into yourself, and then bring it to your daughter or whoever you might be co-creating it with. That crystalline flower is a symbol for you. If you get to a place where you're in the old pattern you can visualize in your mind's eye the crystalline flower and your place in the star-filled field. Focusing on that image will remind the cells of your body what is valuable to you. It will remind your cells of this new choice to live from, the choice to experience the pure beauty of life within you.

Your Soul was very wise to pick a picture that you can easily incorporate. When you hold that picture you are saying to your cells and your world, "This is what I long to know again of the experience of sacred union with creation. I can revel in that and inspire and draw others to co-create from that place in the moment. I don't want to possess or "kill" it. I just want to know sacred union with every aspect of creation. That is a moment-by-moment lifestyle. Then you are creating the deeper, greener place in yourself you longed to know in your heart and Soul.

**Zachary:** Yes, this leads me again to being the real me and letting women be the real Souls that they are. I don't want to possess the women. I want that divine experience, that full-bodied experience, and in the moment I can just breathe it in. And I carry this with me. Good, very good.

**Susann:** You can have that every moment.

**Zachary:** I'm excited now about what I can create, not what I can take from others. I get to experience the sacred nature of male and female being together in this world without taking anything away from another or myself. What a relief. I'm free.

## Finding My Beloved

A majority of those who ask assistance from me want greater abundance in their life on all levels. To want abundance is natural and absolutely aligned with our divine purpose. To want to know love, intimate connection and communion with those we have a Soul connection with is also a natural impulse of the heart.

Since I work at a Soul level, many are drawn to ask me if a Soulmate is part of their Soul path or if I can help them to find the one who makes their heart and Soul sing.

This is a huge and wonderful area of the Soul that is too broad to cover in this chapter. But I can help you to find the way to open yourself to draw this magnificent experience of life to you.

Everything begins at the level of creative energy before it can manifest into the physical realm. To manifest something we must first know what it feels like to have that item or experience. In the realm of Soulmate love this applies very directly.

Why are some people unable to attract or manifest the love they imagine they want even after they have spent valuable time and energy in deep conviction, thought and feeling, attempting to manifest a Soulmate? It's because they are not connected to the energy that must first be held in order to be able to know that feeling and manifest a love relationship.

Many people believe there is no way to know what it feels like to have a Soulmate actually show up. It is all just a fantasy or imagination. They point out that they certainly didn't know that kind of love in childhood, or with any relationship thus far. So how could they know how to hold or feel that possibility except through the vicarious experience of romance novels or movies? Their cells are actually filled with caution at the very thought of receiving what they consciously say they long for.

Because so little love is known, the feeling is that love cannot be trusted. Also, since the only way that person's heart has safely opened to love has been through vicarious experiences, such as watching a romantic movie or reading a romance novel, their heart is open to love only as a fantasy. It doesn't necessarily trust love when it shows up through a real live person. Knowing love only as a fantasy, and not believing real love can be trusted, sends a mixed message to potential partners. This message attracts a potential partner who reflects this level of fantasy love or love that can't be trusted. The cycle of mistrust and disbelief in love deepens. The longing for love becomes more desperate as the belief that love is not possible deepens. This ties into all of our experiences of rejection, unrequited love, abandonment, feeling we are losers in love, etc. Rare is the person who has not held one of these feelings sometime in their life.

The bottom line is this: You cannot experience and, thus, create or manifest, something that you do not believe exists. Therefore, the ability to manifest the deeply longed for Soulmate cannot happen while believing it cannot exist for you. If you do not have connection within you to the possibility of the kind of love you long for becoming a reality for you, are you doomed? Absolutely not! Your Soul knows what it is to know Soulmate love and connection. Your Soul has experienced connection with All That Is. This includes Divine Love. Your Soul also knows sacred union with the beloved Soulmate. All of this has just been disconnected from and forgotten. This knowing has been replaced with fear of love, mistrust of others and disbelief that love is possible. Our challenge is to translate Divine Love into the human facet of love that we long to experience.

The following session gives you a taste of what it is to reunite and merge with the energy and deep feeling connection with the beloved Soulmate you wish to manifest. Remember, as your Soul reunites with this unified field of connection to the beloved, you hold that energy in your personal field and cells to attract and manifest that reality in your life here.

Let yourself merge with the experience revealed in the following session, or use the meditation at the back of the book to guide your own journey to that magnificent space of communion with your beloved. Let the experience fill your heart with the knowledge that you know the love in your heart you have longed for, and can therefore draw to you that reflection of love in an outer partner. Know that this experience of communion you allow yourself opens the way to manifest sacred union with Divine Love in Soulmate connection in human expression.

ᴄ᷄᷄᷄᷄᷄᷄᷄᷄

**Susann:** As we begin, we call in the energy of all that is sacred, all beings of Light who journey with you in spirit.

*At this point Susann leads Lydia in a guided meditation to journey to her Soul-Essence. To follow the meditation for yourself, go to page 229 at the end of the book.*

ᴄ᷄᷄᷄᷄᷄᷄᷄᷄

**Lydia:** I feel like I am walking in a forest and there is a man walking down a path towards me. I want to leap down the dirt path to be in his arms again. He is simply standing there to greet me. Now we are walking down the path and just talking. It's quiet. It's moonlight and we are gazing into each other's eyes and being with each other and there is such a deep communion and knowing each other. I mean everything to him and I can feel that in his energy, and this moment with him is very precious to him.

**Susann:** Take it all in and offer all this energy to every fiber of your being as a beautiful gift of love.

**Lydia:** There's a feeling of our marriage and taking our marriage vows, and they are blending with a few events, the energy of the marriage and the vows, and he is sharing with me that we will always be together. There is an eternal nature to it, not just vows of marriage for marriage's sake. It's a vow of eternal connection and then it immediately overlaps with a time later on. It's like a ripple effect, revealing many times when we are together. He's again offering his abiding, eternal love and presence. And then we do another ritual down the road, to share that and acknowledge that together again.

**Susann:** Just take your time asking if there is more you need to explore, other key events within your life together that need to be integrated and infused with love.

**Lydia:** Family. When we did the vow the second time, there were two small children and other people who were extended family, and the vow was being made on behalf of the love of family and community that we were all sharing. There is a sense of sacred togetherness present. So it wasn't just a witnessing of the vows of us together. We are doing it all together and we are holding a core place for that vow, that all are part of.

And now I'm proclaiming what I proclaimed at that time. There's a symbolism that love will be known for all to be shared and all will be part of it because of our union. The ripple effect will be throughout the Earth where they (whoever they may be) may take that in. It is a vow to love here in this world, through our union and through our sharing it through family and community.

**Susann:** Just feel the power of this energy as it flows deeply through your being, blessing you, filling you with love.

**Lydia:** There's a deep sense of knowing that this was very real for me and that it still lives in my heart.

**Susann:** And, now that you have touched this experience from a previous time, I would like you to bring your attention back to your heart. Feel Light around and in your heart from this experience. Take that Light and also feel Light all around you and let this take you even deeper to the original space where your Soul first knew what it was to be with your beloved. Feel the energy of experiencing the love of a beloved Soulmate. Let yourself go beyond your lifetimes here to a dimension beyond this world, of meeting Soul-Essence to Soul-Essence.

**Lydia:** I see and feel a space that feels like home. When I first come into that home space, there are a lot of little beings that are ecstatic to see me again. And, you know, it is a huge reunion. In a way, I think they show up small because they are like children at one level, happy, playful little munchkins, like some of those fairy-tale things. They are so ecstatic to have me here. I start out very happy to be with them and we are having fun for a few minutes, and then I say thank you but there's someone I need to go see, and I will come back and be with you again. Then my energy changed to a very regal energy, very deep and sacred and at peace. Then he came. The King, the beloved. Then we embraced with total assurance of the eternal nature of our connection and our being together and our love.

**Susann:** Is he incarnate at the present time?

**Lydia:** There is a part of me thinking I can't imagine something of that magnificence being incarnate, a feeling that, "Oh, no, it doesn't happen on the Earth like this." So I have to walk through that feeling in this moment. The King energy is now showing me that he is present. He wants to show that he's down there, so to speak. He had to show me because I couldn't believe it. I believed the only way I could know him was to be in this space with him.

**Susann:** And is there a Soul contract between the two of you to connect within this lifetime?

**Lydia:** The contract was if our hearts moved to that place where our hearts could bear this then, yes, it could happen. If our hearts could hold that space, and if the world could hold that space around us, as we had done before in another incarnation, then we would come together at that time when the frequency was available for us to come together. We left some free choice around it.

**Susann:** Beautiful.

**Lydia:** I know that at least for myself, and I can't speak for him, I had a heck of a lot of work to do to come to this space.

**Susann:** And where are you with that work?

**Lydia:** I'm ready now. That's why I can laugh when I think of the difference between where I started and where I am now.

**Susann:** So take some time to celebrate how far you have come within this life. All that you have learned.

**Lydia:** That's why those little munchkins from my home were celebrating me! Having me back, and being able to hold that vibration here that I knew there, makes them so happy.

**Susann:** Beautiful. What happens next?

**Lydia:** In the home world, we are reuniting. We are doing another ceremony of reuniting this energy field, as it is known there, in that vibration, in that sacredness, and in that purity of love and joy. We are doing a ceremony of acknowledgement that this now can come into the Earth field, that there is a path, or readiness to bring that vibration, to reclaim it and bring that here.

**Susann:** Call in all beings of Light who can assist and empower this ritual in holding the energy and manifesting this pure love.

(A few moments later) Where are you now?

**Lydia:** I want to bring all of this here and yet, at the same time, wanting to be sure I am filled with it very completely.

**Susann:** Feel yourself being filled with the infinite possibilities.

**Lydia:** There's a level of partnership being developed, being taken in that I want to acknowledge…the true vibration of partnership. There's a feeling that now I can be in the world, in union with love.

**Susann:** Take that knowing in. The deep and powerful blessing and acknowledgement, the consciousness of your Soul and your deep alignment with love. What are you experiencing now?

**Lydia:** That is intact and in motion now.

**Susann:** I am currently sensing this powerful gathering and celebration of you, your guides and the universal support of you, gathering to surround you and in acknowledgement of what you have now embraced in body, heart, mind and spirit. What are you experiencing now?

**Lydia:** I'm experiencing the energy of what you were saying about the celebration and gathering, the acknowledgement and support, all connected. I have a sense of a very bright path before me being lit on the wavelength of this energy. It has just been established.

**Susann:** So simply feel yourself on that path, so aligned with that energy, beyond anything you have ever done. The work you have just done has grounded you and aligned you with this sacred path to your beloved. If there are images, or words, or insights that you wish to share, allow that to flow now.

**Lydia:** Yes, there's a phrase. As I start walking down the path, this man appears, slightly dressed like the King, sort of eclectic, but of his own energy. He says, "I await your glad heart." And I am saying, "I am here to take you home." It means bringing that which we knew in that home world here, to take him home and bring him to that place of experience together here.

**Susann:** Affirm that knowing through every cell of your body, every feeling of your heart, every thought of your mind—the deep cosmic wisdom that supports all that you now know to be true.

**Lydia:** I think we have come full circle.

**Susann:** We have come full circle, from an ancient freshness and an open heart. So ask if there is more you need to explore today

**Lydia:** I hear a voice saying, "Be with this one that you are destined to be with. Just be with that energy in the way you have just opened to it so that the fantasy you have held is now a reality. You can have that experience here."

**Susann:** Know that you carry it now, so exquisitely in your being now, so joyfully, lightly and gently. And feel again the celebration in realms of spirit, all beings who journey with you, holding and supporting this powerful manifestation of all that you desire with your beloved.

In this particular situation with my client, Lydia, the physical love partner did appear through a magical chain of events, and the feeling of living happily ever after was certainly present with them when I last spoke to her.

# 11

# SESSIONS ON THE BODY

## Having Real Soul Food

Soul food is made up of all that feeds our Soul. It makes us feel alive, joyful, motivated, assured, powerful and aligned with all that is divinely ordained. It is different for everyone.

At the level of physical food, the kind of food that feeds our body, filling us with a sense of health and nourishment, pleasure, energy and satisfaction, is also unique for each one of us. Yet so many people have problems with food, which leads to weight issues.

Being overweight plagues, haunts and stalks the hearts and minds of so many people. The solution eludes even some who are diligent about exercise and diet. I have explored how this propensity for weight gain is tied into our Soul's expression or, to put it more correctly, the limitation of our Soul's expression through our physical bodies.

What knowledge and assistance would the Soul share if asked how to stop the propensity to gain weight and gain the ability to lose weight? How is the individual longing to be fed and nourished that is not coming through, thereby what is taken in becomes a burden rather than being a source for greater aliveness?

How are we being held back from receiving Soul food—this precious, natural gift of life? What is keeping the physical food we eat from becoming an aspect of our heart and Soul's nourishment and pleasure?

Some have found that even if they eat only celery all day, every day, the weight stays on. There are the endless diets, efforts of discipline, denials, uncomfortable tension around food, and ongoing exercise programs. Some feel that it never stops.

What is it that does not allow us to feel the pleasure of being in a physical body? What sabotages the feeding of our bodies, preventing them from becoming a gift to our heart and Soul?

In so many cases, not only are the "issues in the tissues" affecting the ability to take off weight, or not gain it in the first place, but also the issues lie at the level of the Soul. It may appear that out of the blue you suddenly started putting on weight as soon as you got married, made a life change, had a loss in your life or were under an unusual amount of stress. There are deep patterns that trigger weight gain. These deep patterns will turn everything eaten into a roll of fat at the midriff or on the hips, no matter what we do at the physical level to prevent these weight gains.

As people reconnect to the beautiful, powerful, nurturing nature of their Soul aspects that they have been disconnected from, they effortlessly drop the weight that has been a sabotaging burden, keeping them from knowing their own greatness. They have been locked in a self-absorbed pattern of concern for what they are taking in on all levels, out of fear that it will create the weight they are so tired of having to deal with. As I help them connect with this inherent Soul strength again, the sabotaging issues are disclosed and released. The truer way of being in life is revealed and relived. It's like putting on some new clothes that say, "Yes, this is me, and I love who I am and what I feel like." The old self, the old pattern that had its reasons for holding on to the weight, is dropped in favor of the true way of being in the world. What a relief. What a sense of empowerment, rather than the helpless feeling excessive weight can cause.

The following session is just one example of the path of transformation a Soul journey can bring. In this case, powerlessness was a key ingredient, with other dynamics branching from that core state.

**Beth:** This is really mundane, but my weight is an overriding issue for me right now. Actually, I've been overweight for a long time. I bicycled to the west coast in '87 with a boyfriend. It was fabulous. I was 40 years old and I was in the best shape of my life. But then I went into this depression, a lot of childhood memories came up, I gained a lot of weight, and I have not been able to get the weight off since. I've done a lot of work around the issues that it represents.

**Susann:** Let's talk a little bit about how your concern about your weight relates to your inability to know the true aliveness you once had. We want to uncover what weight is substituting for in you.

**Beth:** I would like that.

**Susann:** You said you were depressed. My sense is that there is a feeling of burden being held in your body. And you mentioned the depression in conjunction with childhood memories. I know that can be very perplexing. Why is it that a small child is so vulnerable to overpowering outside influences? We are so innocent, open and pure at that stage. The depression and the childhood memories combined seem to relate to this pattern of weight gain for you.

**Beth:** I agree. It is still hard for me to comprehend that juxtaposition of overpowering influences in my little life then.

**Susann:** I have found that we have acquired what I call "barnacles" on our Soul before we even came here. Our Soul-Essence has found itself in challenging situations, out of innocence and youthfulness as a Soul. Just as children develop coping mechanisms to help with challenging situations that seem too big or too new for them to handle, so it is for the Soul. Souls are permeable to outside influences. For a Soul, it is just a barnacle, or imprint, that is created by an overpowering influence. The Soul-Essence is not harmed, just tainted. When that is the case, then the imprint comes with the Soul into life expression. I speak more about this is my first book, *Soul Mastery: Accessing the Gifts of Your Soul.*

Basically, what I have seen over and over again in my Soul-level work is that we bring these imprints with us. For you, it was the tendency to allow overpowering influences to have a say in your life. This imprint sent out the signal that you "listen" to others who want to have power over you. In some aspect of you, that pattern is okay.

The good news is, today we are going to change that pattern at a Soul level, where it originated.

**Beth:** That makes so much sense. I've worked so much at the level of my inner child and I still have the weight. I've done the diets, and anything else I could come up with. It can get pretty discouraging.

**Susann:** I understand. It can feel like an endless maze that has no answers and no solution. From what I described, can you see how you were afraid to shine as your authentic, radiant self? An imprint kicks in that says it's okay to give away your radiant, powerful nature. When you were at your best and feeling great about yourself, the pattern kicked in to pull you down and the depression came in. You wanted to hide, so your brightness wouldn't be taken advantage of. This pertained to childhood, and again when you were 40.

**Beth:** Yes, I've always had a little bit of the sense that I don't want to be noticed.

**Susann:** Okay, so remember, talking about the root of the pattern helps to begin to release it. Let's do some deeper work now to reclaim your bright self that is not afraid of being overpowered by outside influences.

**Beth:** That feels right. I want to come out of hiding and stop holding this burden in my body as extra weight. I'm glad we can do something about this pattern.

**Susann:** We are taking a journey to that aspect of your Soul that has knowledge and support of what is true for you. We ask that your Soul guide you in reclaiming your authentic, bright self that is confident and radiant.

*At this point Susann leads Beth in a guided meditation to journey to her Soul-Essence. To follow the meditation for yourself, go to page 229 at the end of the book.*

⌐∽⌐

**Susann:** Feel yourself as a body of Light capable of moving into the dimension of your authentic Soul space, which knows how to hold that space and be in command of your own life.

**Beth:** I feel myself in a pure energy field that is weightless. I like it here.

**Susann:** Tell me more about how it feels to be there.

**Beth:** It is weightless, but expanded. I am still somehow anchored, even though it is weightless. I don't want to come back to this physical body. I'm afraid I will lose this wonderful sensation.

**Susann:** So how would it feel to expand from this place so you can hold both realities? Feel what it is to be in this weightless sensation, even while in a physical body.

**Beth:** I feel like I'm expanding, like I'm in an elevator going beyond the clouds. As I expand, I think I'm leaving my body behind and not doing it right.

**Susann:** Give yourself permission to go to the higher expanse. You're doing great. The true connection will reveal itself.

**Beth:** It's dark now.

**Susann:** Keep moving yourself, surrounded by Light, through that darkness. It is just an unknown space.

**Beth:** I see a shiny gold box, like a treasure chest. I'm finding two keys there.

**Susann:** Remember you wanted to consciously move to higher dimensions so you could connect again to the Soul space of your authentic power. You are being given a key to unlock those higher dimensions. All you have to do is, within your mind's eye, create the visual of the key and say, okay, I want to go as a Soul into the universe. Feel the power of having universal Source at your command.

**Beth:** It's in command and I'm in command at the same time. We are one power source.

**Susann:** That feels so wonderful. Really take in that feeling of the one power source as it lives in your expanded Soul self and your physical self all at once. The universal power supports you.

**Beth:** Yes, I feel that. This is real.

**Susann:** So imagine that at any moment you need clarity and direction. If you need to know, "How do I handle this?" put your attention on this key for clarity, wisdom and knowledge from a divine source. So just hold that key, wherever you want to put it, and bring awareness, Light-filled awareness, to the situation that you wish to bring clarity and direction to.

**Beth:** This is about breaking the chains of my bondage and the sense of having to take care of all this stuff. What I need to do is be an example today in making a statement, and listening to that inner voice and going forward with that. Not so much letting the chips fall but knowing that the powers of the universe will support me and support my Spirit. And leaving behind that fear that has made me so heavy and weighed down.

**Susann:** You feel freer and lighter already.

**Beth:** I am having the courage to trust the higher dimensions because my whole life I've struggled in this reality. How I prayed for this knowledge about true power. I always felt, or I was told, that when I was powerful I was too full of myself.

**Susann:** Now you can feel comfortable being full of your divine essence and full of the universe supporting you.

**Beth:** I feel like I have been two people. This capable person that people respect, and this frivolous person no one understood. I guess I let go of that part and decided I didn't understand it. There went my power.

**Susann:** We're combining power and Light, which is what you are truly made of.

**Beth:** And not to be afraid to be that powerful. I feel that.

**Susann:** You are now realizing that you have these outer capabilities and skills, and you can combine the outer talents and skills with the inner Soul gifts and strengths. Your outer expression is infused with the power of divine Light.

**Beth:** As I feel the universal support of Light in my body, I then feel okay being my true powerful self. Ah, that feels good. I can breathe more deeply and feel the feeling of being that lightweight energy again. Whew, what a relief.

**Susann:** As you let yourself hold this space of power and freedom in your cells, the fears and burdens will fall away.

**Beth:** I can use the key to unlock the old limitations that kept me weighted in this world with the burden of feeling powerless here because I didn't feel understood.

**Susann:** Now you understand yourself and feel supported by the universe. It won't matter so much if others understand your true Soul power. Try that on. Consider your work situation and feel how you feel about it now.

**Beth:** I'm good at what I do. I see that. No one can take that from me. I can maintain this light, free power in my body without having to protect myself or become invisible.

**Susann:** How great. I want you to now take a few deep breaths and bring appreciation to all the beautiful aspects of yourself. Feel the love-filled Soul gifts dancing in partnership with your abilities to be creative and effective in this world. Feel the universal support of Light you have so deeply received, as you move into your life!

## Being Free to Live Fully

The following is a session with a client who wants to work with and release her rheumatoid arthritis. The impact is remarkable and substantial. She describes her experience in her journey to her Soul-Essence through feelings and sensations. This is natural when one is working to release and refresh dynamics within the body. This kind of session can apply to any kind of aches, pains or body conditions. The Soul's wisdom is phenomenal and accurate in its ability to bring new life to areas in us that have stagnated.

**Meredith:** We spoke last time about the rheumatoid arthritis that I am working with. I am *so ready* to be freed up from that pattern. I know I brought it with me somehow, but I don't know what that means in terms of releasing it. I've worked a bunch of childhood issues that seemed to be related, but the stiffness and the pain of movement is still present. Whatever we can do today would be very appreciated. I would like my body to feel more alive and free.

**Susann:** Let's take the journey I spoke about, to your Soul-Essence, to uncover what is creating the limitation and recover the resource that will give you the ability to move your body in the ways you wish to!

**Meredith:** That would put a smile on my face.

**Susann:** I'm happy to help you get that smile back.

*At this point Susann leads Meredith in a guided meditation to journey to her Soul-Essence. To follow the meditation for yourself, go to page 229 at the end of the book.*

**Meredith:** I see a large space filled with a sense of activity.

**Susann:** I'm so glad that shows up instantly.

**Meredith:** Playful, children.

**Susann:** So are you playing or are you watching children play?

**Meredith:** I think I'm watching children play and enjoying it. I now see jellyfish and creatures moving very fluidly.

**Susann:** That's all so fun!

**Meredith:** I see a lot of blue. There's a blue sun.

**Susann:** Anything else showing up right now?

**Meredith:** Yes, stars, only the sky is daylight. It's bright. It's beautiful.

**Susann:** Great. How does your body feel in this space?

**Meredith:** Everything in me feels softer. Nothing is at right angles.

**Susann:** Ah, very nice. So really take in that sensation of your body being in that softer, more pliable space. You are remembering, reminding yourself what your body inherently knows and carries.

**Meredith:** Like Gumby™.

**Susann:** Gumby is that jellylike figure I remember from cartoons. He is made of soft rubber and is pliable and is always smiling. Can you feel the sense of freedom that Gumby carries?

**Meredith:** Yes.

**Susann:** Isn't it fascinating how quickly you went to that true state?

**Meredith:** Yes. Still going, going home.

**Susann:** Are the playful children still there?

**Meredith:** Yeah, they're still playing.

**Susann:** What would it be like to engage with them?

**Meredith:** I would like that.

**Susann:** Good.

**Meredith:** A little bit timid.

**Susann:** Yes, what is that timidity about? Why are you cautious to go into that play mode?

**Meredith:** It seems unnatural. It's not me. It's foreign.

**Susann:** You have forgotten that this is your natural state?

**Meredith:** Yes.

**Susann:** Okay, so take your time with it. Do you need anything to help you with that?

**Meredith:** I have a fear of getting hurt.

**Susann:** Okay, so engaging with others brings up a fear of getting hurt?

**Meredith:** I'm kind of running, and fearful of the group.

**Susann:** So bring yourself back to that softer feeling state of being like Gumby.

**Meredith:** I feel a little rusty.

**Susann:** How is it to be in a group dynamic and keep your own place? Stay with it and see what happens.

**Meredith:** Oh! I got to kick the ball!

**Susann:** Great. Now feel in your body what it feels like to go on with that. Also, feel that your true power is the power of joy moving through your body as you kick the ball.

**Meredith:** That feels good!

**Susann:** Yes! So feel how there's nothing wrong with feeling good. Feel how it allows your heart to expand, and to know love and joy. Feel how the soft Gumby in you allows you to be free to play and enjoy the pleasure of being alive.

**Meredith:** It's hard to keep my size when I feel so Gumby free.

**Susann:** Tell me more about that.

**Meredith:** I have to keep my size. It's hard to stay the size of the kids. I want to be like them but I'm getting larger.

**Susann:** Why do you want to stay their size?

**Meredith:** So I can stay a child.

**Susann:** So, okay, if you start expanding, why do you release that childlike experience?

**Meredith:** I won't fit in.

**Susann:** So what do you have to do to start expanding?

**Meredith:** I have to be a grownup.

**Susann:** And being a grownup means what?

**Meredith:** More observing. I have someplace to go. I am responsible. I stop playing.

**Susann:** Have to be responsible. That is the downfall. Okay, so you just had to separate from that place of joy, of Gumby, because you had to be some kind of adult. So where did this idea come from for you that to expand in your sense of self you had to lose your joyful, playful, soft Gumby self?

**Meredith:** A grown-up council. A group of beings telling me what I need to know to live in this world.

**Susann:** Oh, a grown-up council told you this! Ah, let's talk to that grown-up council. Let's be with that grown-up council. What are they like? How do they show up for you?

**Meredith:** They work at the grocery store and they have white shirts on.

**Susann:** So this is some council you needed to listen to because…?

**Meredith:** I thought they were right. They were authority, they told me. They said I needed them to do life here.

**Susann:** Yes, putting on a white shirt does carry the symbol of having authority! Interesting.

**Meredith:** And working at the grocery store.

**Susann:** So ask your Soul why there was a need to connect with people with this so-called outer authority look.

**Meredith:** Because I thought they had more experience.

**Susann:** More experience in what?

**Meredith:** They told me they knew things I didn't know here.

**Susann:** Do they have that Gumby feel? Do they know about joy and play and aliveness?

**Meredith:** No.

**Susann:** Right.

**Meredith:** Sedentary.

**Susann:** Sedentary, excellent word. This is nothing like joy or Gumby flexibility at all.

**Meredith:** Very different than the scene of the kids playing.

**Susann:** Now let's see what the kids are playing, what the source is that fuels them versus the source that fuels the white-shirt guys.

**Meredith:** Kids are connected to that planet with the blue sun.

**Susann:** Very good.

**Meredith:** I think I want to be with the kids playing on the blue-sun planet.

**Susann:** Do you want to be connected to that blue-sun planet, like it is a source of life and your lifeblood?

**Meredith:** Yes.

**Susann:** So, since you had a feeling of wanting to plug into that, I now want you to feel what you might lose if you're not plugged into the white-shirt guys.

**Meredith:** Freedom to fly away!

**Susann:** So the white-shirt guys who symbolize authority gave you the freedom to fly.

**Meredith:** Yes. But, if I fly, I don't have connection to my blue-sun planet and the Gumby body.

**Susann:** So you made a choice to fly free, but that lost your connection.

**Meredith:** Oh, yes. Now what?

**Susann:** Let's go back to the blue-sun planet where you are with the children playing in the grass. You are feeling soft in your Gumby body and connected. See how you feel in relationship to "freedom to fly" in this setting.

**Meredith:** Oh, the grass is extending. I am kicking the ball. We are playing. The grass keeps extending. We can go wherever we want.

**Susann:** So the Gumby state on the blue-sun planet can actually give you the freedom you were looking for, which misled you to connect to the authority figures.

**Meredith:** Yes. When I listen to authority types my body shuts down. Can we change that?

**Susann:** Yes. That is what you are doing now by reuniting with your original choice: to play and be with the true source of life and loving connection that feeds you, and lets your body feel soft and alive. Feel again what it's like to be in that scene, that state as Gumby, happy and free.

**Meredith:** (After long pause) I have felt the blue energy all around me for the last few minutes. I just get to lie there and be part of that. The blue relaxes my body and helps me come back to that place I love. My body is just buzzing below my waist.

**Susann:** That's so good. Now feel what happens when I ask you about the element of freedom. What happens for you?

**Meredith:** The word makes me want to grow. I feel it as a shift. Lighter.

**Susann:** Check in with your heart and see how it feels.

**Meredith:** My heart is full.

**Susann:** Very nice. Does your body feel like Gumby?

**Meredith:** Yes, my body feels like Gumby now.

**Susann:** Wonderful. You did great.

**Meredith:** I feel great.

**Susann:** Keep moving in this new way of being. It will increase in its influence in your body so the rheumatoid condition can be replaced by the soft, pliable feel of "Gumby-ness" in your body. Visualize that beautiful blue. Feel yourself happily playing with the children. See the grass extending as far as you can see, representing the freedom that lives within you. Keep saying yes to the Gumby, the blue and the playfulness. Say yes to all the Soul dimensions that want to be re-created in you again.

**Meredith:** Yes! Thank you so much.

**Susann:** You are so welcome, Meredith.

## Accessing Resources for True Aliveness

In my session with Joan, the focus of true aliveness is brought forward. We are uncovering one of the ways that our body patterns are connected to our Soul's riches or lacks. This is especially focused here in relationship to the immune system. There is a profound relationship between the function of our immune system and our ability to hold a strong spiritual connection within our body. Health is more than just a matter of physical well-being. Our spiritual health, flowing through and integrated into our body, mind and heart, has a profound impact on our immune system and thus our overall health. Our experience of aliveness is directly aligned with the degree of spiritual resources we are allowing to ignite our physical dimension and our sense of self.

What comes forth with Joan is the direct relationship between a compromised immune system and an area holding a lack of alive connection to her Soul resources. As she reconnects with what it feels like to be fully alive in her sense of self and body, she can feel the old patterns of constriction magically dissolving.

**Joan:** I want to work with the release of my arthritis and psoriasis. I have tried many medical approaches and natural-based solutions that have all been valuable. Bottom line is, I still have it and it hinders my work in the world. It must be a deep-seated issue. That's why I want to approach it from the level of my Soul. My Soul must know what's up and how to help me release this awful pattern. I have learned that the term silent inflammation is what medical professionals believe is at the heart of all disease. In Chinese medicine they would say that there is too much fire in the system that creates the inflammation. It's like your body is in overdrive, or in fight or flight, and when it's in the fight mode the inflammation is created. The body has to back off and back down and get that fire quelled so that there's a balance in your body. You don't want the fire to go totally out, but there needs to be a balance. That's the latest information I have discovered in terms of addressing the physical cause. There's too much fire, too much heat and too much going through the system, so the systems are inflamed. It results in various things, like I have, which is the arthritis and psoriasis.

**Susann:** You would call this an inflamed condition.

**Joan:** Yes. It seems that getting rid of arthritis and psoriasis is a matter of balancing, not putting the fire out.

**Susann:** Okay. Here's what I'm going to say about that. This is the understanding I have come to for what you describe as silent inflammation. Silent inflammation is a result of what I call the "invisible enemy." For example, this concept seemed to come forward after the terrorist attack on the World Trade Center and the Pentagon in 2001.

Our individual and collective fear of some enemy or evil force surfaced and came to the forefront of consciousness. We perceived that this invisible enemy had to exist and was constantly out to destroy us. This was virtually an overnight change in our perception. It had been lurking in our collective subconscious all along, and suddenly the idea that there was some invisible enemy trying to overpower us was in our face and had to be dealt with. The collective unconscious had been holding a fight-or flight-level of survival and now we owned it.

The collective statement, held in our individual cells, was, "Someone else has the power and I am helpless and powerless in relationship to that powerful, invisible enemy." There is a silent inflammation, a fire brewing that is out of control in the system and we are helpless in its presence, except to stay in fight or flight to put this inflammation out. In our session today, we want to work at the level of the emotional fire, the fight-or-flight inflamed response to the invisible enemy. We do that by allowing your Soul to reunite you with your true power source so there is a sense that you hold the power and there is nothing outside of you that can outpower that.

**Joan:** Right. Without that strength, the fire will just erupt again.

**Susann:** Yes. We want to work with the psoriasis. How would you describe what you know about psoriasis existing in your body?

**Joan:** What I know about it is that the immune system is attacking itself. That it's working overtime. It's working too hard. The skin normally sheds cells every 30 days. With psoriasis, however, it sheds cells every three days. So it has set up that activity. It's an autoimmune function gone awry.

**Susann:** So the autoimmune system is saying, "Alert, alert, there's an enemy out there. There's an enemy out there and we have to attack," and there's nothing for it to attack so it has to attack itself.

**Joan:** Exactly.

**Susann:** Okay, so let's look at this function of the skin shedding itself. It's simply on overdrive, shedding every three days instead of 30. Is there anything else you want to say about what you understand around the condition of psoriasis?

**Joan:** No.

**Susann:** What is your understanding about the arthritis you are experiencing?

**Joan:** My understanding about arthritis is that it is an inflammation of the joints. Again, what's causing the inflammation? That's what I want to know.

**Susann:** We are asking your body and your Soul why the joints are inflamed. When the joints get inflamed, what does it limit?

**Joan:** Movement. Grasping things, holding on to things tightly. I can't make a fist. Things slip through my fingers. You can't get hold of what you want. You can't handle things.

**Susann:** So there's a feeling of powerlessness to handle the things in your world showing up in your body. What you choose to handle in life slips away. So you don't feel in command of your life. What we want to do today is to take a journey to those dimensions where your Soul has had experience in holding a place of health and well-being, and reunite this universal connection with your physical being. I would call this the place of true aliveness. You are transforming the feeling of fight-or-flight fire to the pure food for life. This brings the balance in your body you seek. You are using your life force to ignite your creative life choices, not to defend your turf or silently fight off an invisible enemy.

**Joan:** There's an underlying anxiety with it all that I experience. I'm supposed to be doing something and I can't get it done, and I'm worried about it. I'm on this timeline, and I'm running out of time. That's the underlying current. It is a frenetic kind of energy, which I get from this fight-or-flight thing. It hypes me up, and I'm restless and it's hard to focus. It's hard to feel right. It's not going to work. I'm not going to get there is what it feels like.

**Susann:** Now we are going to go to that place where your Soul already knows how to exist in the balanced place of true aliveness coursing through you. We want to re-create that at the physical level for you. Aliveness and life energy already exist at the core of every cell in your body, and outside you in the whole universe. Somehow it has been kept away from parts of you. We want to open the door and allow it to fully flow into your physical being. Now wouldn't that be wonderful, if we could create this opening. We usually call it healing, but I'm going to call it transformation, for this is a transformation in your body to bring it back to the place that it was originally designed to be in, and which you are choosing to reunite with.

**Joan:** That's pretty much it. That's very clear.

**Susann:** I feel like your guides want to help you clarify, transform and be renewed. We will take a journey to your Soul-Essence to reunite you with balance and true aliveness.

*At this point Susann leads Joan in a guided meditation to journey to her Soul-Essence. To follow the meditation for yourself, go to page 229 at the end of the book.*

**Susann:** Let the Light that is present with you now take you to your Soul's remembrance of what it is to feel alive and free.

**Joan:** I see myself on an island and I'm on the beach with a bunch of friends. I feel very peaceful, carefree, with no worries. Everything's taken care of. I don't have to work and I can play. I'm there to play and create. And I'm telling my guides that what I want is to create the same feeling of freedom and being carefree that I have there. I want to manifest that in my earthly body and heart. So my friends and I are sitting near the ocean. It's a starry night and we're around a campfire. We're sitting in a yoga position around this fire. And it's interesting because in my earthly body I can't bend my knees in a yoga position. It doesn't work because the knee joints won't do it. But, there, it's very easy.

**Susann:** And can you actually have a feeling impression of that sensation of your presence there, in this body?

**Joan:** Yes, I feel as if my body could do that. Yes, easily, no effort. Like a doll, you can move it wherever. Very interesting.

**Susann:** So, when you say to "them" that this is what you want, are you talking to your guides there?

**Joan:** Yes.

**Susann:** What do they say in answer to your wish?

**Joan:** They say, "No problem, let's do it." So we just formed a semicircle around this campfire, looking out to the ocean, and the stars are really, really bright, and the Earth is kind of out there somewhere. We are meditating, but sending it out through our foreheads like a ray of energy to make it happen.

**Susann:** And where are you sending the ray of energy?

**Joan:** Out to the universe, knowing it's going to connect to planet Earth.

**Susann:** To the physical Earth world where you also exist?

**Joan:** Right.

**Susann:** Do your friends exist there as well, on planet Earth?

**Joan:** No, totally different.

**Susann:** Okay, like a different tribe?

**Joan:** Yes, it really feels like a tribe. There's really a feeling of acceptance, a closeness, a real bond there.

**Susann:** Okay, great. This ray is coming from them, but it feels like we need to touch into another existence beyond all of you, that feeds all of you, as well. This field of existence of pure creative energy feeds all of you, and all of us, on all levels. Let your consciousness and experience expand to connect fully to all that creative energy.

**Joan:** I feel that space. It is teaming with brilliant Light energy. In it is a myriad of beings holding Light. They want this to happen too. They want my physical healing, because it is all one.

**Susann:** It seems to me that every thing, every Soul, every being in the universe is connected, including every cell of your body, and is aligned with universal life. This universal alignment knows that healing is connected on all levels, in your cells and on planet Earth. Your healing is the planet's healing!

**Joan:** So my success is their success!

**Susann:** Totally, because it's all one mission. Every little piece wants to see all this happen. It makes you remember that we are all part of a huge mission. We have a tremendous force field of support if we allow ourselves to receive it.

**Joan:** Yeah! I want to receive that support, that brilliant Light field, as part of me. It is my food, my divine food. It is what fuels my aliveness. Much better than having the fire of fight-or-flight response creating the silent inflammation that shows up in the psoriasis and arthritis. My body is so relaxed and happy. This is a much better choice of fuel.

**Susann:** Wonderful! I am very happy for this "Soul food" you now have. Keep me posted on how you are doing.

**Joan:** Thank you, Susann!

## Moving From Pain to Pleasure

This session contains a beautiful description of the relationship between our Soul's strengths and our physical reality. In the same vein, you will see how a physical shortcoming, such as a herniated spinal disc, is directly connected to a spiritual gap being held. Carol's reconnection to the missing spiritual resource gives her an instantaneous sense of newfound strength and support. Her body speaks to her through its pain to let her know that the lack of her willingness to go for pleasure and support in her life is, indeed, causing pain that manifests all the way to the physical level for her. The body is her friend getting her attention to awaken to the remembrance of what truly gives her strength in life. A magical process, indeed.

**Susann:** At the physical level, what is happening right now in your back that is causing you pain and the inability to stand up straight?

**Carol:** I have a herniated disc. There is a protrusion in my spine between L4 and L5, which is the lumbar region of the spine.

**Susann:** What does herniated mean?

**Carol:** The jellylike substance between the discs has leaked out from where it should be in fibrous stuff that connects between the discs. The herniation is like a balloon that has bulged out. It is pushing up against the nerves inside the spinal canal, which causes pain radiating down my leg.

**Susann:** We want to be able to get the inflammation out.

**Carol:** Sometimes, due to aging, the jellylike substance, instead of being nice and firm, because of the pressure of the spine, it has kind of oozed out. For instance, if you have a balloon and you pushed it too hard you might have one little spot that would poke out.

**Susann:** Because of the pushing, due to age and some form of weakness that is specifically there for you, the problem has exacerbated. We want to unlock the root cause for this weakness, and help you feed your body with a resource that feeds strength to that part of the body where the weakness has been.

**Carol:** It is in my lower back and has a direct influence on the movement of my hips.

**Susann:** So there is a pressure and strain that keeps you from moving freely. Presumably this weakness has been present and some action took the whole situation over the edge.

**Carol:** Shoveling snow did it. Twisting and compressing did it.

**Susann:** So there is an unnatural pressure we want to take out.

**Carol:** The doctors want me to have surgery to hollow out part of the bone to make more space for the herniation, so the bulge goes back in.

**Susann:** As I see it, the resource you want pertains to space in your spine and the means to create that space where the compression is causing the pain.

**Carol:** If there is space there, the bulge can come back in and release the inflammation, which is pressing on the nerves. I am doing physical therapy, which is useful to pull the vertebrae out a little bit so the herniation can be repositioned.

**Susann:** We want to find out why the body is creating the undue pressure and how it would serve you to create the space.

**Carol:** I do know I have a tendency to push in my life and create unnecessary pressure to make things work for other people, and on and on. I guess that striving creates approval.

**Susann:** I imagine the feeling of a Middle-Eastern belly dancer, in contrast, whose hips just sway easily, conveying an inner state of ease and carefree connection to daily life, with a sort of innate sense of the power of the feminine girdling her life. It certainly conveys a picture that is far different than our "push and strive" Western existence, where we try to juggle marriage, family, career, aging parents, our favorite causes or charities and the faint possibility of a few things on the side that might feed a woman's heart and Soul. So today we want to create a space in you, and the feeling within you that you are not locked into the "drive to survive" mentality that fuels the way you move in life.

**Carol:** I get that. Now that I think about it, I've had this physical condition off and on since I moved to my home here in Boise, Idaho, ten years ago.

**Susann:** So, moving to Boise felt like what to you? Were you excited or anxious? Was it a good idea?

**Carol:** It was a necessary change in our life, for my husband and me and our children. It was for support, come to think of it, which is interesting to consider.

**Susann:** Do you feel you got that support upon incarnating?

**Carol:** Probably not! Especially recently. We came for a job change for my husband, and a better school for the kids. It went well and then my husband lost his job a year ago.

**Susann:** So the family support system changed.

**Carol:** Yes. I do have huge issues around support right now, not just for the family, but for myself personally. It's very interesting to tie these things together.

**Susann:** What we are doing today is helping you to identify not only this pattern of weakness at the emotional and psychological level, which ties into your back pain, but also to bring in the resources at the level of the Soul that can give your back what it needs: space, support and strength that you are lacking and which is being reflected in your back's inability to hold your spine straight, be fluid in movement and keep your hips strong and flexible.

**Carol:** Sounds good to me. I'm curious to see what this is all about, for sure.

**Susann:** We are going to travel to the place of your Soul-Essence that carries the dynamic qualities of your innate gifts that have gotten lost as those qualities have come into your life and especially into your physical existence—very specifically, into your lower back.

As we go to this place of Soul-Essence, be aware that your Soul wishes to take you to the place that it knows well. It is a place that will feel natural to you in your deepest cells and will feel part of a larger, spiritual, even universal, orientation.

*At this point Susann leads Carol in a guided meditation to journey to her Soul-Essence. To follow the meditation for yourself, go to page 229 at the end of the book.*

**Carol:** I feel like I am on a place that is purple, with mountains and four moons.

**Susann:** How does it feel in your body when you see all of this?

**Carol:** Kind of a peaceful feeling. Restful. This is home.

**Susann:** Breathe that in. Let yourself relax into it more deeply. And, as you take that in, does anything else present itself to you at this time?

**Carol:** I feel like it's a still, peaceful, marshy place.

**Susann:** As you walk in this space are there other aspects of life with you, or around you?

**Carol:** There is the Light from the moons.

**Susann:** Is that comforting to you?

**Carol:** Yes.

**Susann:** Is there a sense of spaciousness in this scene and in this home place? Can you move naturally in this space?

**Carol:** This is really strange, but the feeling I get is that this is where I am from, this is my origin. The very dirt or base, somehow.

**Susann:** The very substance out of which you were formed, would you say?

**Carol:** Uh-huh. I see it as the root of creation for me.

**Susann:** The four moons you mentioned. What is your relationship to them?

**Carol:** It is where the energy comes from. They are harvest moons.

**Susann:** So they generate brightness of presence?

**Carol:** Yes.

**Susann:** Knowing all of this, what would you say is your job or purpose in this space?

**Carol:** Being in the origin.

**Susann:** In this place you get to be the originator of creation the way you choose it to be. You are in command. Does this feel true for you? How does it feel that you are in charge and you get to use all these ingredients, such as the dirt, the moonlight and the purplish mountains? I see them as celestial ingredients. How does it feel to choose to have all these ingredients available to create with, as you wish it to be?

**Carol:** So far it feels like all of this just happened. I'm not really in charge of anything.

**Susann:** That is excellent that you recognize that. Would you like to change that, so you can feel in charge again of your existence, and thus your life now?

**Carol:** Yes. There's a big difference between being the victim that just lets everything happen, and being the one in charge of my life.

**Susann:** Just take a moment to be with that insight.

**Carol:** Maybe that is the issue, that I just go with the program.

**Susann:** When you "just go with the program," it often means that you are going with someone else's program, in fact. This is in high contrast to being the Queen of your existence with the moon and stars and the root of creation all around you, supporting you. This is okay, for it is our divine birthright for each of us to say, "I am the Queen of my existence and I am in command of what I wish to manifest in life." This is not selfish, since it is connected to your divine roots and comes from the voice of your Soul.

**Carol:** I get it.

**Susann:** Feel where you are now. Be in that feeling of "it's just happening to me." Feel your relationship to these moons. What is your relationship to these moons?

**Carol:** They are the energy and they give the energy freely.

**Susann:** They give this energy freely as support to all that you are and all you create.

**Carol:** Yes.

**Susann:** Let's get you connected to the energy of being the creation of your world. Remember this is your Soul's original stance. What do you need right now to strengthen your Soul's connection to being the creator of your world?

**Carol:** I guess I need to own up to being in charge. That it's okay to do that and I will be supported for that. Okay. I am rising up as a Queen-like figure now.

**Susann:** And what gave you the power to do that?

**Carol:** The moons and my decision to be it.

**Susann:** Why did you decide to be Queen-like?

**Carol:** Because I want to be powerful.

**Susann:** Why do you want to be powerful?

**Carol:** So I can take charge of myself.

**Susann:** Feel yourself connecting with that Soul-Essence place inside that is ignited and energized by the moons and is all around you.

**Carol:** That place starts to expand because of all those cosmic ingredients supporting its growth.

**Susann:** How would you describe that place?

**Carol:** What it comes back to for me is the feeling like a place of birth.

**Susann:** Wonderful. Feel yourself being birthed, on your terms, in your time, and let Light be the energy that births you. How does that feel?

**Carol:** It feels empowering; it comes right in.

**Susann:** Okay. So there is a Queen presence that feels empowered. How does that feel in your body?

**Carol:** My spine is straighter.

**Susann:** Feel what your heart is holding. Feel the quality of the change that this Queen presence brings to your heart.

**Carol:** Stronger. My heart feels strong.

**Susann:** Now let it go into your abdomen.

**Carol:** It feels like it's clearing. It's more energetic.

**Susann:** Describe what happens when that Light comes to stay.

**Carol:** Yes. A little looser, a looser quality to it.

**Susann:** Now let's go to your back.

**Carol:** It feels like more Light in my spine—silvery blue Light.

**Susann:** Okay, from this space look at your world. You can keep your eyes closed. Notice aspects of your world. Is there anything at all you notice in your current life situation that might not support you being in that Queen-like, powerful, Light-filled space?

**Carol:** Yes. It comes back to the theme of doing what is expected of me and not really knowing what I'm supposed to be doing.

**Susann:** Excellent. What you want to do now is start being the Queen. Feel what it feels like to hold that sense in yourself. Come from the Queen posture as you step into and walk into your life. You haven't known what to do because you've been in this mixed place of responding to others. When you come from the Queen place, you'll be able to start to generate what's true for you. Do you see what I mean? Before you couldn't hold your powerful self. You came from the collapsed place before, so to speak. Your job is just to hold this place without thinking, "Gee, what am I supposed to do, what's my job or purpose, especially according to others? My job now is to be Queen for my life." Every time you think of that word, then that energy goes into your body, the silver blue goes down your spine, and the space comes in from the Light of home. Then you want to see those moons, and the purple mountains, supporting your Queen here. Then you are pulling in the Queen quality that says, "I'm in charge of my life." Feel the support from your Soul-Essence to be who you truly are.

**Carol:** That's interesting.

**Susann:** Remind yourself, particularly when you're at home and around your family, that this is what matters. You are training your body to respond to that and create from that place of being straight and strong. And then part of your visualization, meditation and work around your spine is going to be to visualize the silver blue Light and the moon energy going into the spine. You can feed that whole sensation into your spine, and into your hips, particularly. You can also do the journey we just did in the last few minutes in your meditation, as well. Let the new sensation into your heart so you are acknowledging that it feels good to hold this new energy in your body.

Let the silver blue Light flow through your whole body to repattern the nervous system and all the cells to this new position. You are saying to your body, "This is the place I live from." Just keep repeating that declaration as you breathe and move and live your life. It will move the energy and strength and reality of that declaration into your cells. You will begin with directing those words to your spine. Then you will pronounce those words with your focus of attention on your heart. Notice how doing that helps you feel even stronger and more upright. Then you will allow the energy of that declaration to move into your abdomen, to support the strength returning to your spine. Just keep holding this feeling of this place you live from to allow your body to repattern to this new place of being and moving altogether.

**Carol:** Queen-like! I feel I can move again, but not as a Queen who sits stiffly on a throne but a Queen that moves at ease around her kingdom.

**Susann:** I am reminded of the song from the movie *Pretty Woman*, called "Wild Women Do" by Natalie Cole. This is a great line for you: "…What you only dream about, wild women do…" It feels to me as though you are moving out of the dreaming phase to the action phase of being the Queen, not one of the others who only dreams.

**Carol:** I like that. I will have to look up that song, and be the Queen dancing to it. Fun.

**Susann:** While you are being the Queen, you can bring into your consciousness people who hold this noble, regal place to you. In any moment you can have a quick image that stimulates the cells of your body to love being the Queen of your wonderful kingdom. Then you can do anything else for healing in the physical plane, whether it's physical therapy or massage or whatever you choose. Just remember when you are receiving these services to include in your awareness the sense of creating that magical, powerful place of home in your body.

**Carol:** I think I've got it.

**Susann:** Yes, I think you do.

Following our session, Carol attracted an osteopath and a physical therapist, both of whom have proven stellar in the support of her healing process. They have helped her strengthen her physical capacity to hold the Queen energy that is her divine essence. They have been an essential ingredient in the team she is creating to support her ability to hold the Queen energy in the home of her body.

From Carol (Four months later): "My wonderful osteopath and physical therapist have been very helpful. The emotional and spiritual piece that was revealed in our session has been a cornerstone to my healing process. The value of this work has continued to show itself in many subtle ways since then. At this point I can honestly say this healing process has been a gift in reuniting me with my true Queen essence. And I really enjoy the fact that I can feel supported in holding this genuine stance in my body and in my life."

# Having a True Life-Support System

Two years ago I worked with a client in relation to his strong feelings of exhaustion and lack of motivation. We discovered that these feelings related to his inability to be clear about his job direction. He came to me to help him make choices regarding his career options. As we spoke, we discovered that his inability to make choices directly related to his lack of motivation to move forward in his life. What happened in his body as we spoke of his feeling of lack of motivation in any direction was fascinating. His diaphragm cinched up and his abdomen got tight and constricted, like it was shutting down. He felt the exhaustion that was held deep in his bones, which he hadn't been so keenly aware of before.

This is a common occurrence in a session. The body is such a tremendous barometer for what is going on with us emotionally.

At the heart of any form of exhaustion is the lack of life energy being brought to where it is needed to feed the necessary energy field and physical body. It could be at the place of motivation to move forward in being productive, or in the desire to get out of bed in the morning ready to greet the day ahead, or it could show up as an illness as complex as chronic fatigue syndrome.

In our Soul-Essence journey we discovered that an essential umbilical cord to his Soul-Essence had been cut off. He had connected this life-support system to other endeavors outside himself to support their purposes as more important than his own, in the name of service. Consequently his life force was being siphoned off, by choice. He felt lethargic and unmotivated for the fulfillment of his own life purposes. This pattern kept him from wanting to fully engage in his life. We repaired the leak by reconnecting him to his Soul's natural umbilical cord. He then had his own life-support system fully intact and engaging on all cylinders. He was a new man.

He hadn't felt he deserved to have the powerful life that was his Soul-Essence destiny. "What about the starving millions? If I am coming to this world to help, don't *they* come first? Who am I to be powerful, successful and revealing of my brilliance?"

We all can answer those questions for others, but holding them as true for ourselves is another story. As soon as he felt the universal support that was inherently present when he aligned to his Soul-Essence and purpose, he felt to be his authentic, powerful self.

When I asked him the question, "How do you now feel about bringing all that you are into this world?" he gave an enthusiastic, "Great." He almost surprised himself. And, as we brought this new energy and reality into his abdomen, he felt a relaxation happen in that area where it had been constricted.

We reinforced the connection when the feeling came up in him that said, "I don't know if I can do this." When I listened more deeply, what I heard him really saying was, "I don't know if I can do this alone."

Excellent. That's true. So we deepened that sense of umbilical connection from his Soul-Essence to the place of restriction in his throat and abdomen so he could have a sense of support where it was needed, and know he could do what he needed or wanted to do with the support of the Soul-Essence umbilical cord feeding his life needs.

We also worked with his sinus congestion that related feeling unfree to breathe the breath into his life. We created an umbilical cord to universal life breath. The freedom that came into his face was visible. Then he was able to get clearer direction about which career choice was a match for supporting his life movement and Soul-Essence purpose. It was a wonderful turnaround.

Any place of physical limitation you see and feel within yourself can show you how "tired" or shut down it is due to missing a true life-support system.

Take your own journey to your Soul-Essence to bring your umbilical cord of life into direct connection with your Soul-Essence. The place within you that is feeling tired, unmotivated, withdrawn, stiff, stuck, even frozen, will shift. Notice the Light fill your body with a necessary, sustainable, reliable Soul-Essence infusion of aliveness. You are bringing those Soul riches to your life.

# 12

# SESSIONS ON CREATIVITY

## Living From Limitless Possibilities

Whether we are feeling the urge for a new work situation, or a greater depth of connection with a partner or loved one, or whether we are sensing that there is so much more that we have yet to experience, the field of limitless possibilities is a vital one to take us from where we now are to where we wish to be. Simply to take in the feeling of limitless possibilities in any moment is a breath of fresh air. To feel that we could live from the place of limitless possibilities is truly cause for celebration. Our Soul is quite naturally connected to the field of limitless possibilities; so, too, can our outer sense of self be connected as we take in what it feels like to exist in this space of freedom, where creativity is always at our fingertips.

The following session is an example of a man's experience in opening that field very specifically for himself. It can assist you to have that blossoming for yourself and your creative endeavors.

**Susann:** What do you think prevents you from having happiness?

**Raymond:** Those things that are the "trash" of life. You focus on things that have happened, things that you are worried about that are going to happen, future responsibilities; and I think the sort of negative effect is that it creates barriers about being really focused on right now. All those things that keep me out of now. I can tell that the "trash" makes me feel limited and unable to go where I want to go in consciousness. Like feeling really happy. The limitations in my head keep me from that freedom space that gives me that authentic happiness. I try to keep "taking the trash out" because if I don't it turns to fear and frustration. My ideas get buried by the trash, so I doubt my abilities. When I find myself "in the trash," I try to do the mental mantras that I say to myself and speak of my thankfulness, to focus back and get the trash moved out, and then kind of get centered into "The time is now, the place is here." Happiness for me has been trying to be consistent with this process and not see so many obstacles out there.

**Susann:** Thank you for updating me on your process. I like what you've been doing.

**Raymond:** I do too. And at the same time I know I want to really expand my definition of happiness and what is possible in my life. I feel like there's a ceiling on what I am able to connect with spiritually. That's why I'm here. To expand not only the sense of potential, but feel much more in touch with what my Soul has in store for me. How do we go about that?

**Susann:** You are in the right place. We want to take a journey to your Soul-Essence so you connect with the feeling of happiness that I hear you desire to know in a larger sense. We will "download" what your Soul is already accessing of the limitless possibilities for creation that you can tap into. This true sense of freedom is the expanded space of happiness you are seeking. I would love you not to have to work so hard to focus on "taking the trash out" and repeating mantras all the time. It feels like keeping your finger in the dike to keep the floodwaters from overtaking you.

**Raymond:** I like that thought. Ease is good.

**Susann:** As you hold the feeling sensation of knowing the quality of happiness that is true for you, it streams into your body and radiates into your life. The trash is automatically emptied for you because the happiness has more value in you and takes the place of the trash you had to be so mindful of before.

**Raymond:** Now we're talking. I'm on board for this one.

**Susann:** I heard something recently that reminded me that it really is okay for each of us to feel so good about our connection to universal wholeness that we can say we are "God Almighty" or "I am in heaven."

**Raymond:** I think that's great. It certainly is a matter of choice.

**Susann:** For you, here and now, I sense that it would be great for you to be able to proclaim that you are happy because you feel it in your very bone marrow, and not because you are good just at managing the trash.

**Raymond:** It has been really good to be on top of things this way, which is all part of taking my power back. And now I am ready to take my process to a new level. I guess to a Soul level.

**Susann:** That's exactly right! Your Soul knows what can be opened up for you right now. We may call it happiness, but I sense that at the level of the Soul there are expanded dimensions of limitless possibilities wanting to be gifted to you. Let's allow that wealth of spirit to be engaged right where you are. Let the journey begin.

*At this point Susann leads Raymond in a guided meditation to journey to his Soul-Essence. To follow the meditation for yourself, go to page 229 at the end of the book.*

**Susann:** As the Light surrounds you, let your Soul take you to the space that you desire to expand to at this time.

**Raymond:** I keep having an image of a place that keeps coming up called Standing Rock in an area called the Maze in Utah. It's a wonderful place and it has a sense of vastness beyond my comprehension. The times I've been there it feels like a portal to greater awareness. And there is an immense rock that rises up many stories. I have always slept under it, and when I sleep under it in my tent, it's where I enter it as a portal. The shadow of this rock is incredible and massive. I always remember crawling into my sleeping bag and being there. There's a sense of leaving all of the temporal stuff behind, and I feel more comfortable there than in any other place in the entire world. It's always been a portal where I experience a total release of the limitations of the dimensions we live in. And portal is the word that strongly comes to me.

**Susann:** Close your eyes and go into that portal. Imagine yourself going through that portal into the vastness. Standing Rock is an embodiment of this vastness for you. When you touch Standing Rock, you go into the vastness of the universe that you already exist in. So let yourself go into complete expansion as though you're just taking a spaceship into outer space and leaving this temporal stuff behind. It's important for you to feel that you have permission in your daily life to go to expanded states within yourself while functioning at the temporal level. This journey helps you to feel okay about what that looks and feels like for you. And it shows you how it enhances your life.

**Raymond:** It's a wonderful place.

**Susann:** So, in that vastness, have you gone beyond seeing Standing Rock? I want you to even go beyond. Standing Rock is a symbol. Go into the feeling behind the portal and let it be a pure experience of the vastness.

**Raymond:** There's a sense of being a spirit, just an immense reaching to the omnipotent.

**Susann:** Yes, limitless possibilities.

**Raymond:** There's a passage through the portal and then a wave comes out and there's literally universes of all kinds of Light and colors and swirls and comets, and Light! It's like fireworks but with a calmness.

**Susann:** Yes, calmness and creation happening all the time and fireworks of energy movement.

**Raymond:** Yes, that's a good point. It's like going down the rabbit hole. There's a whole lot happening.

**Susann:** Now that you are in that space, close your eyes again because I want you to experience within your body that universe of Light and colors you were just in. Where you are could be called the land of manifestation, and this is where all creation starts and anything is possible when you're in this space—anything. It is the energy field of limitless possibilities.

**Raymond:** There's a sensation of a sphere that I feel right alongside of my ears. I feel a sense of letting go and I feel a sense of the excitement of possibilities.

**Susann:** So let's touch into the nature of the sphere that just showed up. If you go into the space, what would you say that you are afraid of that might happen or might not happen?

**Raymond:** Failure.

**Susann:** Failure. In what dimension of reality would failure happen?

**Raymond:** On the other side of the portal. It is not part of the vastness but is trying to pull its way into the scene.

**Susann:** Okay, so how can you just move the sense of failure out of the scene? It's present but just sort of hovering, saying, "What about me, what about me? You've paid attention to me, you said I was important, now you're saying someone or something else is?"

**Raymond:** That is really just like that. What I've been doing in my current life is embracing the anger toward having that fear. Now I am saying I just won't let the sense of failure have that power anymore. I know that it is self-created and we're just going ride down and grab it and stop it. And I know it may come back tomorrow, next week or next month but, finally, it won't even come around.

**Susann:** So what I want you to do is go into this vastness. Now, when you feel the fear from the place of the vastness, feel where it is in your body physically. Is it below the belt or above the belt? Just get a sense of this. There you go. Now just start breathing into that area. When the fear comes up, you can know it comes up at a time or in a space in you where the vastness is not lived potently and powerfully, so it makes its little way in because there's a weakness due to the lack of connection to the vastness there. Breathe in the vastness to create the power resource you are looking for, as it helps release the protective barrier that the fear has created in your body.

**Raymond:** There's a calmness now.

**Susann:** Okay. So this is an exercise that is going to be very important for you to start to use. What you were using before to push out the trash in your head was great, but this is going to allow it to be a little more thorough so that the fear doesn't come back. There won't be a place for it to come back to. When you push it out but don't change the vibration in the heart, it comes running back, "We gotcha!" Now you're changing the vibration in the heart and it's like, "Oh, there's no place to go, we can't get in there."

So now go into that vastness again. Here is an important addition I would like to bring to you. Call in your guides or higher self or Soul to give you an impression, a symbol, a sensation that represents absolute connection to this vastness. This symbol allows you to maintain and hold sacred, absolute connection to this vastness for you.

**Raymond:** A very strong picture of Light.

**Susann:** I want you to put a slight sensation of Light around the vastness. Now bring that stream of Light around your heart so that the vastness is always surrounded by this strong sensation of Light around it as it streams into your presence, heart and body. See what that's like.

**Raymond:** There's an image of Light in this form of guiding Light, showing the path.

**Susann:** So Light is giving direction to the vastness. The Light gives the energy of right action into which the vastness can be channeled. This allows the vastness to direct your life. We want this vastness to have a place at this level of creation.

**Raymond:** I just got an image of a compass.

**Susann:** Cool.

**Raymond:** Which is something I really enjoy touching and working with. It's one of my most favorite tools to work with. I love what a compass carries.

**Susann:** The compass is good. It can be held like a gauge within you. So, if you're doing something in the world that doesn't have a connection to the vastness, doesn't have Light as part of it, you sense the compass directing you not to move forward.

**Raymond:** The compass seems to be a great tool. If I try to follow it, the Light becomes brighter, and if I try to move out of the connection, there is dimness.

**Susann:** Right, because it's not guided by Light and Light is connected to the vastness.

**Raymond:** I'm not afraid of the unknown, if I have my tools.

**Susann:** Excellent. It has to be that way. Our fear of the unknown comes from our disconnection to spirit and its guidance.

**Raymond:** Literally, I am feeling a very, very strong burst that I really, really want to go down this path. Right now, I have this huge sense of, "Just Go!" It's almost completely overwhelming.

**Susann:** That is the sense of true power. Now feel what you are feeling as a sense of power. Being connected to the vastness of limitless possibilities is the true sense of power. We could use the phrase I mentioned before here. You are now "God Almighty" for your world. I'm "God Almighty" for my world and this is my kingdom. There's nothing wrong with holding that true sense of power.

**Raymond:** It's in the most humble sense. It's a privilege to have this awareness. I really don't want to lose this image.

**Susann:** You want to keep bringing this in all the time because it's so real. It's becoming a part of you.

**Raymond:** Right, I want it to be me. I want to be it. You mentioned the word powerful. Over the past week, especially when I finished doing yoga for an hour and a half, as I was walking, I could feel everything in my body in the most intense way—taking a simple step, walking down the stairs. I had this sense of enormous power. Not evil, just an awareness of the infinite part of me at its high point during those times. And it just felt so good! And there was kindness and gentility.

**Susann:** Yes, the heart comes along because you are engaging the heart in the power. The kindness, the humility, the sense of privilege is part of the power. When the heart is not engaged in power, that's when it's off. It's not true power.

**Raymond:** I'm feeling like that now.

**Susann:** Now what we're going to do is to add some more icing on the cake. Go into the vastness for a moment. What you're going to do when you're in that vastness is to ask to be given the key to the essence of what you are calling "happiness." See what you're gifted with to be able to help manifest more happiness in this dimension. See what the vibration of happiness carries for your Soul, your heart and your self.

**Raymond:** It's really easy. I want to bring where I am back with me.

**Susann:** Great. I want you to feel the vastness. Breathe it in into your whole body, and you can do it gradually or at whatever pace you want. Start with your throat, your heart, or just let it stream all the way in. Let me know when you have it throughout your whole body.

**Raymond:** Okay, I'm there.

**Susann:** Okay, now feel what you are calling "bringing it to others." Feel yourself radiantly holding the vastness. You're just radiating vastness. You don't have to bring it to others; you don't have to give it to others. Just radiate it like you are a sun. And for those who choose to be with you in that frequency of radiance, they are going to say, "I want what he has," and they will open themselves to it. Those who don't, won't, in varying degrees.

**Raymond:** Oh, I see a metaphoric image of a higher place and a lower place. I'm here and I would have thought that I would've needed to come down to the lower level to provide what I know here, but I don't need to. It's here with me and that is all that matters.

**Susann:** So does the sun come down to Alaska because it's a little bit colder in Alaska and there is a special need there? No. Thank goodness, because it would melt Alaska. So the sun simply radiates.

**Raymond:** That's a big shift. I can't rescue anybody. You can put all that energy into rescuing somebody else, you lose it. You take yourself out of that place.

It's a choice to be at Standing Rock, or in the portal. This is what it means to have limitless possibilities. From the field of limitless possibilities I am happiness. Happiness is me.

**Susann:** Yes, this is a much more expanded view of happiness than we might have believed.

**Raymond:** Yeah, really. Now I feel like I could just take a nap.

**Susann:** That's terrific. Something in you can now deeply rest.

**Raymond:** I feel a sense of beings, maybe guides, smiling.

**Susann:** That's a wonderful picture to hold when there's something difficult or tense. "I'm surrounded by a field of smiles and happiness."

**Raymond:** That's exactly what this feels like. Like they're all anxious to start down a new path that the compass prescribed. The path doesn't lead to a place. Being on this path, in that vastness, with this awareness holds a choice point. Where do I want to go? I feel good. I feel like I could pick up my backpack and do or go anywhere, and still continue to hold this power of unlimited possibilities.

## Having the Freedom to Create

Free choice in life is a wondrous dimension, but it carries many challenges as well. Many feel the constraints of free choice rather than the freedom free choice brings—that we can truly create whatever we wish to create in any moment. When we live outside ourselves, as in living for others or for outside influence, such as approval, acceptance, love, etc., we consequently release our inner freedom to express ourselves according to our heart's pulsations. We lose the sense of freedom to create in our lives because we feel tied, albeit unconsciously, to live according to the dictate that our needs can only be met by factors outside ourselves.

The freedom to live from a place of free choice comes from the ability to stay true to our heart and Soul and be fed by our Soul's resources rather than be fed by that which is outside ourselves. It does not mean we don't thoroughly enjoy every aspect of life that we encounter that comes to us in the spirit of co-creation with us. Our ability to move from the freedom of our Soul is the means for true freedom each one of us knows is our birthright to experience.

This particular session is with a woman who has had numerous sessions with me around a common theme, so she was very ready when she first got on the phone to bring a fresh, Soul-level perspective to the whole topic.

**Sally:** I hold a sense of being defeated, and I feel like the goals I remember that I set as a kid are not going to happen. Anger comes up—such anger at all those who created the obstacles. I don't approve of myself because I couldn't overcome the feeling of defeat as a child. I wish I were proud of something I have done. It's familiar to feel defeated. I couldn't stop the abusers when I was a child. Even my goal to just *be* a child was defeated. Now, as an adult, I want to feel proud of who I am and I want to believe in myself. I don't know where this deep sense of feeling defeated came from. Will I ever be able to get over this huge hurdle that makes me feel so pinned down all the time?

**Susann:** Believing in yourself is essential to any realm of manifestation. The abuse you have had in this lifetime comes from the place you carried in your Soul that says, "I will be defeated, no matter what I do." That opens you up to allowing that belief to materialize. If you are abused as a child by a relative, family member, neighbor or child-sitter, they are attracted to that weakness in you that says, "I will be defeated." In essence, they play the role of the one who defeats you, the one who keeps you from being your child self. Your freedom of spirit, your creativity, your playfulness, your joy, are defeated. You give parts of those elements away to the one who plays the defeater in your story so you can hold the belief that you will be defeated.

Instead of going to the scene of the crime, so to speak, trying to undo the abusive scenarios, we want to take you to the place where your Soul knows how to take you beyond this defeated place you have held yourself in, to the place of feeling successful in all you create, as a child and as an adult.

Every Soul knows how to create what it desires. The Soul is given the tools or training to be able to create and manifest the physical existence it chooses, and then bring to fruition all its plans and purposes. When the Soul's voice is given the opportunity to be heard, creation burgeons. So we are going to journey to your Soul-Essence, with the specific intention of reopening your connection to your ability to be in command of all that you choose to set up and create in your life.

*At this point Susann leads Sally in a guided meditation to journey to her Soul-Essence. To follow the meditation for yourself, go to page 229 at the end of the book.*

**Susann:** Let the brilliance of Light take you to the space where your love knows how to create from limitless possibilities.

**Sally:** As I touch into the space that is the home space for my Soul, I feel a sense of joy. I can be happy. I have freedom to create what I want. Then a voice comes along that says, "Forget that. Life is about getting the food on the table." To this voice my purpose is inconsequential. I have to do the material world and I'm supposed to forget the joy in that, which my Soul knows is the necessary spiritual component for life. Somehow I feel like I have to do my life according to the way it is done here to make it work here. "When in Rome, do as the Romans do," is the phrase that comes to mind.

**Susann:** I can see where you felt defeated from the very beginning if you didn't feel your joy, or your love to create, was welcome here. Your sense of mission to bring that joy and freedom here with you was defeated and you felt you needed to listen to and follow the rules of the herd mentality to survive.

**Sally:** I felt there was no way of getting anything done in this world. Even right now, as I'm thinking of this, I am fighting the feeling of being a victim. I don't like that feeling, but I sure don't know how to get past it. What could I have thought of? What plan could I have made to avoid this happening? I wish I could figure out what I could have done differently. I feel like there was no way around this.

**Susann:** I understand your dilemma. You have learned to use your mind as a coping mechanism to come up with plans in hopes of avoiding these feelings of being defeated. I want you now to feel how it feels in your body when you hear the voice that says, "Forget the joy part. All you can do is make sure you have food for surviving. There is no room for creating. You are already defeated in that." Feel what is happening in your body right now as I say that.

**Sally:** My heart constricts and I feel a general shutdown, or wanting to shut down out of fear.

**Susann:** So all you have left when your heart is constricted and your body is shut down is to go into your head, which is your coping mechanism to keep you safe from this fear-producing voice that seems always to be around. Then the mind makes a plan to help you make some sense to your life.

**Sally:** I get that. I forgot to listen to my heart and body. But I didn't know how to help them when they were in a constricted, shutdown state.

**Susann:** Remember that when your heart constricts and your body shuts down your Soul and innate wisdom have very little means of coming through to your consciousness. You end up operating from a fearful mind, which is a fraction of your resources, if you could even call a fearful mind a resource. You ask yourself, "Why was I not able to come up with something to overcome the defeating voice?" The fearful mind is not capable of that task. That is why we are reaching for your Soul knowledge in how to handle the situation.

**Sally:** I see. Because I went into using a survival tactic to meet this outer threat, I ended up playing the survival game.

**Susann:** When the heart is closed, there's no room to create divine connection and, therefore, have the inner strength to create what is true for you, regardless of what the world around you is focused on.

**Sally:** I became very isolated and had to go with "their" plan, which became the abuser's plan in this lifetime, for the sake of survival. I also became an empty shell. There was no resource I could tap into to help me deal with this situation back then. I was separated from all my resources and capabilities. Wow!

**Susann:** So let's go back to that first Soul connection space you made a few moments ago. Feel that space of joy and freedom to create what you want.

**Sally:** Okay. I like this better.

**Susann:** Really sink into this large sense of joy and happiness permeating all of you. Feel the connection you have to the Divine that supports your joy and creation. Sense the world before you, virgin like, as a place to step into from this feeling of joy and connection remaining intact. Feel how good it feels to have all of you engaged in this way.

**Sally:** It feels like I'm just on a totally different plane than anyone else. Others around me on the survival plane are just focused on getting food, and I'm sitting there feeling that, yes, I can focus on my need for food and I can also bring joy in life. Others are looking at me like I am nuts, but I don't care how they feel because I feel connected. I have purpose and I feel very whole and alive. They are wondering why I'm not struggling like they are, even though we are both looking for food.

**Susann:** Let's recall that feeling of isolation you had before that made you feel you had to play the survival game so you wouldn't feel isolated. Now to play with this I want you to imagine yourself on a football field with all these football players coming at you and you are the one with the ball, attempting to go in their direction. You freeze and shut down and forget. You forget to look to either side and say, "Oh, my gosh. I have a team here with me. There are people all around me on my team, supporting and backing me and my purpose to deliver joy." When you came here it felt like it was you, holding joy, against the multitude, just surviving. When you shut down you can't see with the vantage point of your heart and Soul. You can't see who is also here on your team, wanting to create joy. You couldn't possibly be the only one, even though it felt like it in that scary, shortsighted moment.

**Sally:** It's about a choice of who I take into my heart and who I don't. You can take in your team, but not those who aren't already connected to joy.

**Susann:** It is wiser to go to the place where joy is received and honored.

**Sally:** I see how I can attract new people into my life that honor my joy. Instead of being a missionary in life, which gives myself away all the time, I can enjoy my life and then share the joy as I go. More rewarding for everyone, I would say. I would much rather attract people who are interested in life than those who want to defeat it. Just attempting to survive seems like a way of being a defeatist to a real, joyful life.

**Susann:** We are helping you feel that joy *can* be received here, and does not have to be defeated by those around you and by the belief inside you that says it will be defeated and you have no choice in the matter.

**Sally:** I see how I am realizing that living for others keeps me small and unfulfilled. Then I have nothing to give anyway. Aha!

**Susann:** You can forgive yourself. You carried the pattern of feeling defeated because, when you came here, you didn't see any way that your joy would be received. You forgot that you came here to bring joy and hold it sacred and valuable by giving it expression, not by tucking it away, or giving it away and emptying yourself of it. You can simply forgive yourself by letting yourself experience the joy of life now because you are alive.

**Sally:** I have the choice. That's freeing. So the question is, can I set a goal now and feel it's possible to fulfill? My answer to myself is that it is not the goal that is so important, it's enjoying the process that is the so-called goal.

**Susann:** You are establishing that place inside yourself as you described it earlier that says, "I am proud of who I am and it's okay to create from that place of confidence."

**Sally:** If I stay in that place, that inner foundation will move me toward my goal; I will honor myself and not put out self-defeating roadblocks.

**Susann:** The truth is that your Soul agreed to live as joy and, therefore, you bring it wherever you go, which happens to be here right now. Your Soul did not say, "I'll bring the joy, and if they like it, I will be fulfilled and happy, and if they don't like it, I won't be fulfilled."

**Sally:** I can see that for me, with the myriad of creative projects I have, what really works is for me to simply be able to create. It doesn't matter what the project is, or what the goal is, I just want to feel free to create.

**Susann:** Let this be your goal: to keep your state of heart and mind and body continually holding joy and the freedom to create. As you are mindful of that, as you check in and develop the feeling of joy as the new pattern in your heart, the freedom to create will take hold and take off and everything you do will come from that place of creation. Your Soul will naturally be fulfilled and only those who also are joyful and free will be reflected in your life.

**Sally:** I can feel that, and I'm very excited to play again and retrieve my joyful, childlike nature that makes me feel really good. Thank you.

# 13

# Sessions
# on Transition

## Meeting Your Crossroad in Life

All of us, at some point, find ourselves at a crossroad in our lives, wondering which road to take. Maybe this happens for you frequently. So many voices, inside our heads and from those all around us, provide possible direction for our road, our life ahead. How do we get in touch with the right choice, the best choice and the most appropriate choice? We are typically surrounded with more options than we can deal with, leaving us with an overriding feeling of being overwhelmed that paralyzes us from moving forward at all. Forget about even just taking a first step. Our crossroads in life are crucial junctures in the unfoldment of our life purpose. I work with many clients who ask me what their life purpose is. They also come to me looking for assistance in how to take the leap from their job to their Soul's work. They want to know how to open up the field or area that makes their heart sing so it can be their life work.

Listening to the voice of your Soul in the matter at hand can be refreshingly helpful. It is a voice you can trust because it has your best interest at heart. Robert Frost said it so aptly, "two roads diverged in a wood, and I—I took the one less traveled by, and that has made all the difference." This less-traveled road often is discovered by listening to the Soul's voice that opens up a door not previously considered but is true from the perspective of your life purpose.

The following session describes a prime example of this scenario that Robert Frost described. This client's journey was filled with an uplifting, clarifying, expansive path opening ahead for her.

**Susann:** Tell me what brings you here today.

**Betty:** I feel restlessness deep inside myself. It is somehow related to my choice of not having gone into a professional career as a concert cellist. It seems as though life keeps giving me an invitation that says, "Do you want to take this opportunity this time? Do you actually want to enter a competition so that you can step into this career that you have decided not to pursue over and over again?" The restlessness around this is about me feeling that I have this great gift, and the frustration I feel about my hesitation in going into a more formal, traditional concert situation when it presents itself, as it is now. I don't get it. There is such a dilemma here for me. I don't want to be a thoroughbred, but I do have this enormous gift inside that I want to use and express myself through. Another part says, "Maybe you did choose wrong. Maybe you should have, in the past, chosen this path of the traditional performing career." I have a lot of conflict in my heart. It's a tear, almost. So there's an identity attached to the idea of the performing career. I just can't understand what that's about.

**Susann:** That's a very good description of where you are internally. So, as it relates to having an enormous gift and then wondering if you did the right thing, can you feel back for me to the first time in your life that you were engaging with the cello, engaging with being the persona, the identity, of a cellist and how it felt to you then in those very beginnings?

**Betty:** Let's see. I would say I was 12 years old. I liked the feeling of the instrument. It was like the beginning of a relationship. I was also quite intimidated by the power of it, and my first teacher was a real taskmaster. He tended to be very hard on me and didn't understand my heart at all. I rose to the occasion, but it was a very strict discipline of learning the mechanics of the instrument. I loved the instrument.

**Susann:** What drew you to the cello?

**Betty:** I think it was my dad and my competitive nature. My mother introduced me to the piano when I was seven or eight. I remember thinking that there were too many people playing the piano and I wouldn't get anywhere with that one. I felt I could get somewhere on the cello. There aren't very many people playing it. I liked the challenge of learning the cello because it was much more complex an instrument than the piano. So the motivation for learning came more out of my head at that point.

**Susann:** What was your heart feeling when you were going into this place in yourself of strategizing, being competitive and having a strong drive to excel?

**Betty:** It felt very good and exhilarating. I felt able to take it on.

**Susann:** You felt very competent at that young age to take it all on.

**Betty:** "I can be the best at this," is what I felt at that early stage. Of course, then, I didn't need to break it down and figure out how it was all going to come together and work out.

**Susann:** And now feel yourself moving along from this age and strong beginning and sense when and what pulled you back from being fully in that arena.

**Betty:** The strength of the drive kept going through high school. I performed for thousands of people for the high school graduation and I loved every minute of it. It wasn't even scary. Actually, at the high school recital, I was scared. I had to perform on my own for the first time. I felt scared and all alone. I was doing it all by myself, on a stage all alone.

**Susann:** So the translation for you from that fear-filled recital was, "If I step into that field I will be very alone."

**Betty:** Yes!

**Susann:** Okay.

**Betty:** Afterwards, the positive feedback was so strong that I just kept going. But I think the fear created a damper in my heart around the drive. So that is when I chose not to pursue a concert career. I had auditioned all over the country and was given scholarships and I chose to go to Missouri. I was looking for the teacher that was going to help me. It was when I got to Missouri and found this teacher that I became rebellious and said, "I'm not going to do this. I am not going to be a thoroughbred." And ever since it has been like that. Then a spiritual quest began to happen, and that had more impetus for me than a concert career at that stage.

**Susann:** So in back of the rebellion was the fear of being isolated if you kept this thoroughbred drive going.

**Betty:** Yes, anytime I have played in more traditional venues, that's what happens. The talent becomes what is seen, not me.

**Susann:** "If I become this thoroughbred, I lose my sense of self." So you began to feel that you weren't going to do this "show" for a teacher or anyone else.

**Betty:** Exactly.

**Susann:** So your desire to have *your* life and not be on the path that others were heralding for you and which, at the same time, you feared would isolate you, set you out on your spiritual path.

**Betty:** Yes. I see how I wanted to find what was really true for me that wouldn't make me feel lonely.

**Susann:** Who I am, not who do they see me as.

**Betty:** That's right. Absolutely.

**Susann:** What it looks like you are doing now is saying, "I have this talent and I know who I am. How do I marry the two without being thrown back into the arena of what others want me to do with my talent?"

**Betty:** Maybe it's more like, "Let's finally look at this issue and clarify it." I am willing to move into this arena as long as I know who the allies are and who the enemies are. In fact, I want to have this arena open up. I recently was in Seattle in a concert performance, where I have been before, and there was such a heartwarming sense of many allies there. Many who loved my talent and got me and saw me for who I am, not just for what I can do. It was thrilling and very scary for me.

**Susann:** You were seen for the wholeness of you.

**Betty:** Yes. And there was a real connection between performer and audience. People were actually moved and inspired. That means a lot to me when people are touched. I don't want to be oohed and aahed just for my skill. To me that doesn't move people. It is just an intellectual experience if they see only my expertise. It is obviously important to me to have our hearts meet and be moved.

**Susann:** So what we are doing now is defining "What I want and how I want it to be." So you can now create it in the venues that work for you, drawing those situations to you that reflect who you are and what you want.

**Betty:** When I think of this competition coming up my rebel comes out. I want to fight this crazy, driven format being placed before me.

**Susann:** What I want to help you see is that even though the rebel looks like it is hindering you, there is truth in back of that rebellious expression. The rebel is the guardian that says, "You don't mess with me." And, "It's my life."

**Betty:** Absolutely. I know that. And how can I put my rebel into a place that functions healthily.

**Susann:** We will also bring in the frightened part that is afraid she will be isolated if she stands out for her talent and is not seen for who she is.

**Betty:** Thank you. Sounds great.

**Susann:** So now we are going to go into a deeper place to access the resources we need to really take you to where this restlessness wants to take you. Also, listen to what your Soul wants to say to you about this crossroads and what wants to be brought to you for direction and clarity in your path now.

*At this point Susann leads Betty in a guided meditation to journey to her Soul-Essence. To follow the meditation for yourself, go to page 229 at the end of the book.*

⤶⥈⥉

**Susann:** Let the Light move you beyond this space, time and dimension to the dimension of your Soul-Essence that has always existed, and hold the knowledge that you need for this time in your life now. Feel what it is to move into that space with any impressions, feelings and natural images that are showing up for you at this moment.

**Betty:** It's like a bubbly spring. Very peaceful.

**Susann:** Are you watching the spring, or are you part of it?

**Betty:** I'm part of it.

**Susann:** So it brings you peace. Does it bring you anything else?

**Betty:** It brings me joy. I can hear the sound of the bubbling spring, that life-giving essence. The air is very clean and fresh.

**Susann:** Are you alone?

**Betty:** Yeah.

**Susann:** And does that feel okay?

**Betty:** Uh-huh.

**Susann:** Do you feel alone?

**Betty:** No.

**Susann:** Imagine that this wellspring, this life-giving essence, can live with you all the time. You said that you felt a part of it. Feel what it is like to consider bringing this essence of you into your life here. This essence is an aspect of you that has not been fully available relating to your career path, as you would like it to be. So this is an opportunity for you to connect with this essence of a wellspring of peace and joy and bring it to this crossroad in your life. This essence is a resource to give you clarity of direction for your life steps ahead.

So now let yourself embody this essence and see or feel yourself coming back, to this world. This time the peace and joy-filled wellspring within you comes also. Take your time to birth yourself into this Earth, filled with this gift of you. Bring this precious nature of you with a sacred sense that it stays intact as you consciously imagine a reentrance into a womb space for the birth of this expanded sense of you.

**Betty:** It's the same. It's like sparkling water. Calistoga. There's a sparkle to it.

**Susann:** My sense is that the sparkling water, the sparkle, is an activation of life force within you.

**Betty:** Yes. A yellow-white color, like a column through me.

**Susann:** What would you say it gives you as you bring it into this dimension?

**Betty:** The same essence. Not so much peace, as happy. More activity to it.

**Susann:** Now what we are going to do is to allow you to create various scenarios, and see what it feels like to touch those scenarios from this place. Let's start with age 12 for you.

**Betty:** Yes. I think what it feels like is wishing there was someone who could have guided me in the depths of me, like the 12 year old with a teacher, or during the solo concert. If there had been that level of guidance, it would have been a very, very different experience.

**Susann:** What we will do is let that guidance feel like it is present in your cellular memory. How would you like to bring the presence of the guidance you wished to have with you at those times? Do you imagine this guidance in the form of a recognizable figure, or an inner sensation?

**Betty:** An awareness of this column of Light within me feels like that does it for me.

**Susann:** That column within you, does it extend beyond you? Is it connected to anything beyond you?

**Betty:** It is connected to a feeling of a larger Light. I don't have a definition for it. I just feel it. It allows everything to align.

**Susann:** Let your body rest in having that present with you as you move into this field of performance that is so important to you.

**Betty:** Okay.

**Susann:** In your younger years you went into playing the cello based on your compulsion to strategize and compete. How do you feel now with this new resource, this column of Light within you, about your talent, performing and moving forward in this field?

**Betty:** It just feels natural. It is just a wonderful way to express. In a way the strategies don't matter so much. It feels like a very obvious way to express, to express myself in this plane.

**Susann:** Can you feel your heart connected to and aligned with performing?

**Betty:** Absolutely. I love it.

**Susann:** Feel how good and natural and true this alignment is for you. When you are ready to move to another scenario, let me know.

**Betty:** Sure.

**Susann:** High school. Solo performance.

**Betty:** It feels so simple now. The solo concert feels like, "Of course. This is how I am here."

**Susann:** Present tense. What do you feel around your present set of choices at this crossroad in your life?

**Betty:** That still feels unclear.

**Susann:** Tell me about that.

**Betty:** Because as soon as my mind kicks in I get confused.

**Susann:** So when we go into the present tense you need to go into your mind. You can't stay in the place of the wellspring of peace and joy. The column of Light takes a back seat.

**Betty:** It takes more to hold it. I get scared.

**Susann:** The mind seems to hold a place of protection for us when we get scared. So, being aware of that, feel yourself being even more deliberate in holding that column of Light for yourself as you declare that you are reprioritizing. This part of you that is scared of being alone and isolated can feel the comfort of the wellspring and all that comes with it for you.

**Betty:** Okay. Now I see myself in a recent performance in Chicago.

That feels so good. It completely resonates.

**Susann:** Excellent. Now consider the competition that you are potentially taking part in that is on your plate right now.

**Betty:** When I view that, I'm scared. There's a sense of, "Am I able to do this?"

**Susann:** So let's go back to holding that place of the wellspring column of Light holding/being the guidance for the depth of you.

**Betty:** I feel like in the arena of the competition there is no space for that guidance. The inner guidance I have now says that arena cannot honor this depth of me.

**Susann:** That is wonderful to feel that accuracy.

**Betty:** It's not present there.

**Susann:** So when you hold that Light within you that allows you to feel someone is guiding you, that guidance says that to go into that competitive arena is like going into a lion's den. This does not mean you are pulling back, merely listening to your fear. You are listening to the inner guidance to direct your outer life. This outer arena does not reflect this inner space you honor. This is what needs to be heard in your heart and followed.

**Betty:** You know that competitive arena is not designed to reflect that Light. I'm sad about that. It is a kind of letting go of that kind of scenario.

**Susann:** You are actually sad about letting go of the need for task-masters directing the expansion of your talent. That is all you knew when you were young. You thought that to be in that arena, those types of people had to be there. And you now know that can't work for you. For a part of you there is a sense of loss. Rightly so.

**Betty:** People I have really admired for their skills and the way they have found their Soul calling are those I feel I'm letting go of.

**Susann:** You long to find that Soul calling for yourself. You know that you have to have this guidance that can hold a place for the depth of you, as well as honor your skills. You have to be in the settings that bring this forward.

**Betty:** I'm sad that this can't happen in the setting of the competition.

**Susann:** If you had someone in the competition who really understood you, how would that be?

**Betty:** It doesn't matter. It's not about that. This arena doesn't reflect who I am. It's not going to happen there.

**Susann:** Okay.

**Betty:** I think the fear now is around the unknown. If it doesn't come in the obvious ways, how is it going to come? How will I use this instrument? I have had such a love affair with that instrument. Now what will work?

**Susann:** So let's go inside and feel this Light within you, connecting to the cello and feel that relationship again. What would it feel like to have the two of you within this wellspring, bubbling into life?

**Betty:** Well, I'm back to square one. I want to play my own stuff. I love expressing through that instrument. I love having the freedom to do what I really want to do and say through the cello what I want to say. At a Soul level this is what I have come to do.

**Susann:** And can you feel that this Divine Love and connection is at a much deeper level?

**Betty:** It's at a deeper level, yes. Absolutely. I feel that. It helps. Now it is more that I think I just need allies.

**Susann:** Allies to help you with the ability to bring this expression into the world.

**Betty:** I know that one ally has just shown up. She is relatively new on the scene, but I know she is there for that reason. I think I can bring in another person.

**Susann:** Consider all the people who have been with you in recent performances. How can they be allies for you now?

**Betty:** That's a very good question.

**Susann:** How can they further birth that which is important to you? They truly see you. They are reflectors of this guidance system for you. So you are at the place of feeling, "This is what I deeply want to do.

Who wants to back me in this?"

**Betty:** That's exactly it. I'm convinced of that now.

**Susann:** You are the one that defines how your talent will come into the world, not some established system of people.

**Betty:** That's right. I feel that deeply. I just wanted the backing so I wouldn't feel alone. They were the ones that appeared.

**Susann:** And now you know what you truly need and the kind of people you resonate with and resonate with you.

**Betty:** What I need is someone, or ones, in a practical sense who would promote me.

**Susann:** You are putting it into the energy field now that this is the equation that works for you, and you are going to ask the universal Light support, that you are connected to now, to have the right people find you and you will find them.

**Betty:** I get that. It's very strong now. I was waffling before.

**Susann:** This is so good.

**Betty:** It's going to work! Thanks.


In this particular situation the crossroad showed up with pleasant surprises for Betty. Life does not seem to show up in the simplicity of black and white. It is usually far more complex than just the "…two roads diverged in a wood," as Robert Frost described it.

This session was an opportunity to see beyond our mind and emotions, which may see only two choices. It can feel like there is a ping pong match going on in our head, as we bounce back and forth between "Plan A" and "Plan B" in our mind and heart. In this case, the wisdom of the Soul shone a light on "Plan C."

In Betty's case, Plan A was to do what she loved, but this plan was fraught with the sense that playing the cello in a conventional, standardized performance setting wouldn't allow her to feel seen in the depth of who she is. She would be seen merely for her outer talent. That felt unsatisfying and undoable without selling her Soul. Plan B said, "Give it up, because if you aren't seen and understood, why torture yourself?"

The Soul confirmed Plan C, which said, "Yes, you can marry your talent, which you know deep within is your gift to this world and the avenue for peace and joy to be known in your life, and your desire to be supported by allies who support you and see your beauty on all levels." In Betty's case this meant she could play her own compositions and open herself to the allies that would bring this easily and magically into being.

Since then Betty has had a number of people show up to be the outer reflection of her inner guidance system of the wellspring of Light. Performances of the caliber that she envisioned have occurred regularly.

As you find yourself at a crossroad, wondering which road to take, be open to a whole new avenue appearing which your Soul wishes to provide for you, one which takes all the factors into account and then generously adds the wisdom of the Soul perspective to the equation. The Soul also gives you the energy, motivation and practical connections needed to get the job done.

Keep listening as Plan C unfolds, revealing what your Soul wants to share, and keep letting your Soul know you are ready to receive the next set of instructions, each step of the way.

# Making Career Choices

I worked with a man who was in the midst of creating a new job after twenty years in elementary education. It was summertime and he was having a grand time playing and taking advantage of this two-month break. Alongside this spirit of adventure he had a feeling that kept creeping in that said, "I'd better get on this job search." He put his ad on Craig's List but received no responses. He began to feel the crunch of time and a money shortage looming. He began to feel his internal struggle getting louder. "Should I go for what I love to do and have a passion for, or just compromise and get a full-time job with benefits that at least pays the bills?" This is such a common dilemma many find themselves in throughout their lives.

He said to me during our session, "If I do what I love, the job that I want to create may not show up, or no one will want to hire me, etc. But if I settle and compromise, I'll be in the same boat I was in for twenty years. I'll be in a job that left me drained and feeling useless."

We identified the two voices in him, dancing in the struggle: the part that wanted to live passionately and creatively, and the voice that wanted to be sure to have a job and benefits, not a money shortage. Back of the voice longing to be passionately creative in his work expression, was a fear that he would die with his song unsung and never really get to fully live. Back of his voice of fear, concerning compromise and money shortage was a fear of dying, plain and simple.

It was time to connect with his Soul and get a better perspective on how to handle this dilemma. Two distinct paths showed up for him. We took a journey to be with his Soul-Essence and see what his Soul had to share. Also, it was important to help him deal with the fear that had him paralyzed and made him unable to choose either path.

We discussed that in his Soul memory was a belief that to even come into life meant he would lose all connection to the Light of his Soul. He found himself terrified about coming into the world and saw himself in the cold, dark, cramped space of his mother's womb, feeling a sense of impending doom, with even a sense of death all around him.

It was very scary and confining for him, and he felt it was no way to be in life. He realized that in a deep, deep place he felt that to live equals death. He perceived that to come into the life he knew here, all manner of limitation and failure would be with him.

So we asked his Soul to give him a better way to approach life, so he could live creatively and love what he does *and* be able to make the money he needs to truly love life and not just survive. For him survival equaled dying slowly.

The Soul reminded him of the connection he always had to a constellation of Light that appeared as stars that carried the feeling of true family connection. This sensation made him feel fully alive and filled with a renewed vision for coming into the Earth. He journeyed to Earth, this time filled with this resource for his life. This time he was dedicated to bringing this constellation with him, to hold the vision, the support, the love and the connection he needed to live from his heart, and his desire to live from his vision, knowing he would be taken care of. He now embodies a sense of magical purpose that is unstoppable.

He brought all of this experiential sensation with him during our journey as a tingling in his cells. He felt fully alive and this time he did not drop this connection when he came into the Earth field. The first time around he had dropped the connection in order to feel a sense of belonging in this world. At that time he took on this belief that life equals death, and you can't create what your heart and Soul chooses but must succumb to surviving, at best.

Not this time. This time he soared in with confidence that his creative talents would be received here and he would be rewarded for them. He held the constellation of Light within him and all around him that proclaimed throughout his tingling body that life will prevail, while he felt the Soul support surrounding him and enabling him to feel assurance in sharing the magic of himself in his world.

I spoke with him a few months later and was not surprised to hear him enthusiastically describe the new job he had landed. He was alive with possibility as he stepped bravely into this new world he created.

# 14

# Session on Life Purpose

## Finding My Life Purpose

Anyone who has found themselves opening to their Soul's call to awaken to Spirit's part in their life will find themselves asking the following questions. What is my life purpose? What have I come here to do? I know there is something more for my life than mere survival. That is what got me started on a spiritual quest to allow my Soul to give me direction and answers, rather than just my parents, or society, or those self-sabotaging voices in my head that seem to stop me rather than encourage me. I want to make a difference. I want to contribute to the upliftment of this world and those in it. How do I discover the best way to go about opening that path that is true for me and my Soul?

I address this vital consideration in depth in my first book, *Soul Mastery: Accessing the Gifts of Your Soul*. Here is a taste of what it looks and feels like to deepen and clarify that guiding Light within yourself so that your sense of value and direction can be known, and also given a sense of divine commission.

**Eloise:** Ever since I was in Egypt a few years ago, I have had a few déjà vus that I would like to understand further. Actually, it happened when I was in Egypt too. I saw one of the statues, the lion-headed Sekhmet, and I felt she was alive. I found myself walking exactly as I had walked to the site eons ago. It was as clear as watching a movie to see myself in that previous time.

**Susann:** So you had the sensation of your time there, not just an image.

**Eloise:** Yes, and in doing that I was watching myself.

**Susann:** You mentioned you've had other similar experiences since then.

**Eloise:** I've had a number of them, and I had one the other day. I had an issue with a friend of mine, Carolyn, who tends to be self-absorbed. The way that plays out is that she will make a commitment and then just spontaneously change her mind because she wants to do something else, without really checking in to say, "Is this okay?" It just kind of happens.

**Susann:** You mean checking in with herself, or with you?

**Eloise:** Checking in with the person involved. This is what happened the other day. A group of us were going out and she was planning to drive. None of the others could drive. When the time came to leave, she decided she wanted to go ahead because she wanted to go shopping afterward. I've known her for years and years, but recently I've been realizing that this behavior is having an impact on me and I was angry. So I thought, gosh, this is really interesting. I wonder why I'm having such strong feelings about it.

We all went to a daylong seminar. And so we got there and we were talking about our experiences, what we're learning, or what we're noticing, and whether there was a shift and anything was happening. I'm sitting right across from my friend. And what I'm seeing is my friend and I as priestesses in some kind of situation where part of our initiation was to go to the underworld. I could see it, I could feel it, and it was a very different kind of experience and sensation. Very hazy, in a way.

We were in the underworld, and I know it was very important to the whole group that we were a part of that we come back from the there. I saw Carolyn getting farther and farther away, more and more enamored by what was going on there. She got spacier and spacier, which is exactly what is going on with her Soul now. And I am really getting concerned about her. The farther and deeper I went to retrieve her or try to bring her back, the more I knew that it was going to decrease my ability to reemerge to the surface and the Light.

And so I was in such turmoil. It's the same feeling I have now. How could I leave her, and what would it be like to go back without her? I knew, for the sake of the community, that I couldn't just leave her. And so what I found I could do was give her a Light that we both had brought with us, some kind of Light quality that was physically manifested. And hers was nearly gone; there was not enough for her to get back. So I gave her a piece of mine. She's not even seeing this Light, or even interested in trying to find her way back. I felt like I had given her all that I had to give, and then I left to come back.

**Susann:** So the feeling was that you were able to give her what was needed for her to make a choice, based on Light, and then you were free to do what you needed to do without the feeling of leaving her behind, in the dark, so to speak.

**Eloise:** Yes. It was an intense and amazing kind of thing. It's had a big impact on me. I feel free. I'm done with this! So my question to you now is, does this déjà vu experience with Carolyn and our group being priestesses in the underworld have to do with my Soul, who I am, and what I'm doing in life now? What's the meaning?

**Susann:** I see that through the experiences you are describing to me you are rediscovering another aspect of yourself in another dimension, another time frame. By going into the past to a time when you had the resources you needed to take care of the need in the moment, you're able to tap into these resources to benefit your life now. Is that a clear way of describing it?

**Eloise:** It is! It's perfectly clear. And, also, it feels like parallel time. Like you were saying, "Yeah, that's the past but it's happening right now too. So then it's kind of confusing because it's all the same. Maybe it's something that's in the future. But it's not, really. It feels like it's parallel, somehow. I've heard that terminology, parallel existence. But I certainly never applied it to myself.

**Susann:** In the past few years, I have been discovering, more and more, that we are tapping into a parallel aspect of ourselves that already exists, to allow us to resolve what we are feeling unresolved about in this lifetime. This parallel aspect is in another dimension, the dimension of our Soul's essence, where everything is whole and complete. We are going into that place, that sensation, where the solution already exists. Is it past, future, present? It seems to blend into one undefined continuum.

**Eloise:** Very interesting. Deep inside I know what you are saying.

**Susann:** Yes! This is great that these parallel dimensions are opening for you to use.

**Eloise:** You know, Susann, I do think that I have had some sort of connection to the parallel dimensions because I did spend a lot of time alone as a child, and I would say that I did hang out in other spaces. I spent a lot of time there, actually, now that I think about it.

**Susann:** I see what you are describing as hanging out in other spaces as an ability to be in an expanded state. That is what we all want when we say we want to have spiritual fulfillment while having the joy of a human existence.

**Eloise:** And it's not something that I was ever inclined to talk about at all.

**Susann:** So then you didn't feel like it was very real. And you are here to have this all feel real and be validated for you.

**Eloise:** Exactly. But when I was sharing with the group what had happened, when I saw myself as the priestess going to the underworld and all that, they asked how I could be sure if it was real? I told them it was as real for me as you and me sitting here talking.

**Susann:** The truth is, your anger towards Carolyn shifted. That's what matters. The proof of its reality is that it shifted who you are and how you view the world. And that's why it's got to have some kind of reality to it, because it's taking you where you want to go. That experience makes it real.

**Eloise:** The anger resolved because I went back into the previously locked-up situation and unlocked it. That simple.

**Susann:** When we bring Light into a situation where it was missing, it transforms the situation.

**Eloise:** Yes. Well said, thank you!

**Susann:** You are welcome. I am glad that some of your true gifts are surfacing so that you may recognize what you have to bring here that may have been somewhat covered up.

**Eloise:** I would even go further to say that throughout my life I've thought, "Well, what is my purpose here? What have I come here to do?" But I could never really satisfactorily connect with the depth of that until recently, when I did something that related to healing, and even more than healing, to transformation. But I need to understand how that applies to my life and my desire to serve and be of assistance, but not in the old therapeutic ways.

**Susann:** That's excellent. So now it's a matter of seeing that your purpose here is to transform all that you touch in this world through the power of Light.

**Eloise:** Yes. Yes. Right, I want to serve, and transform.

**Susann:** What keeps you from letting that purpose be clear in you?

**Eloise:** The idea of service, of being a person who is available and doing service, really was distasteful to me a number of years ago. For one thing I felt I had been in that position as a child growing up. It was expected of me, and I was at my mother's "beck and call" to the point where anything I accomplished, or anything I did, really only had merit as a reflection on her. So it really wasn't mine; it was for her. It used to be that if I saw anyone was needy at all, I just didn't want to be there. I'm starting to have a totally different feeling about that.

**Susann:** Okay, I just feel all sorts of great things coming out of this time together. This is wonderful. And what I'd like to do is just a little bit of a journey to your larger dimensions so we can really establish this purpose for you, and you can have it permeating every moment of your life, rather than just showing up sporadically.

**Eloise:** So it rings true to you?

**Susann:** Absolutely.

**Eloise:** It's really nice to say it too! To claim and to acknowledge, not just to be doing it quietly within myself, but to share it with you!

**Susann:** There's something wonderful about being able to declare it, describe it and state it, which is all very important, and which definitely brings your sense of self and purpose to a new level.

**Eloise:** Yes, really nice.

**Susann:** Okay, so we're going to take a journey to an existence that your Soul knows holds your sense of purpose, alive and well and strong for you, so you can access it with gusto.

**Eloise:** Okay. I'm ready for that.

*At this point Susann leads Eloise in a guided meditation to journey to her Soul-Essence. To follow the meditation for yourself, go to page 229 at the end of the book.*

**Susann:** Feel the Light taking you into the parallel dimensions. Take your time and let yourself move easily into that space that your Soul knows well. Be with that parallel dimension as it wishes to reveal itself for you now. When you are ready, you can describe that to me.

**Eloise:** Magic! It feels like an energetic field. Pure. Magic.

**Susann:** Do you see any forms or structures within this energetic field?

**Eloise:** It's interesting. If I look with my eyes, I can see something manifesting in the energy field. But it all starts as Light and then takes a form, somehow. If I look and wonder, "Are there flowers?" then it would look like flowers, but it would be Light energy.

**Susann:** But you have enough definition that you know it's flowers versus teddy bears. But the dominant characteristic is that of Light.

**Eloise:** Yes! It's amazing.

**Susann:** So, when you thought the word flower, the Light transformed into a flower. So you are seeing the energy field out of which the flower is manifested.

**Eloise:** Exactly. It's an energy field called flowers, if you want to call it that. But you know it could be anything. That's just one thing, flowers.

**Susann:** This is fantastic. As you play with it, see if you can sense how this relates to your life's purpose.

**Eloise:** It relates because that's just who I am. I see that I am nothing more than that manifestation. I am an energy field.

**Susann:** Wonderful!

**Eloise:** I am an energy field that has the ability to transform whatever it is that has an obstruction energetically, to bring it back into unity, and back into that Light.

**Susann:** To bring it back into its original nature.

**Eloise:** The only nature that is really real!

**Susann:** So you are seeing that everything first began as Light before it took on a unique form.

**Eloise:** Light is a creative fire for manifestation.

**Susann:** Very nice. As you are in the creative, energetic field, what do you see as your purpose there?

**Eloise:** It is nothing more than to vibrate with the creative fire. I don't really have form, but if I look to see where I am then I have form, and I can see that all it looks like is the form that would be Eloise, but the form is just formed by that Light. It's resonating and vibrating in the same kind of creative fire that the flower does, the walls of a building or even the ocean—everything that I look at.

**Susann:** What does your presence bring to that picture? How do you assist?

**Eloise:** Play. Creative fire.

**Susann:** You ignite creativity with the Light of fire. Would you say that's true? The play is the creative juice that helps to ignite the formation of the flower. Your consciousness takes it from presenting it as energy to presenting it as a form.

**Eloise:** Yes, exactly.

**Susann:** Your presence there says, "Let there be flowers."

**Eloise:** Uh-huh. Yes.

**Susann:** So how can you apply what you just touched into and created to what you're doing in your life now?

**Eloise:** Well, the first thing that comes to my mind is that being here and having that awareness gives me the feeling that this is so much my being that there's no way I can be here without bringing this to every moment. And, when I bring that here, I may see others with their problems, but at the same time I see or feel their essence, beyond the problem.

**Susann:** It's like seeing their pure existence. You are saying, "This is who you are and this is how you first existed; and, therefore, seeing that truth in you, I can help you bring it forward again." So you are seeing from the eyes of the Soul. You are seeing your world from a Soul level.

**Eloise:** Wow!

**Susann:** Is there anything else you want to share from this space?

**Eloise:** Holding that space for someone doesn't feel like any effort at all. It's quite something.

**Susann:** Or reconnecting to the essence.

**Eloise:** Well, I think it will be very interesting to see, no matter where I am, how this will have an impact. I can apply this in lots of ways.

**Susann:** The fun will be in your new ability to come from this new perspective of being in the creator field and being able to take on your rightful purpose again. See how it enhances the way you walk in the world. This is something any of us can do. We can't change somebody else's way of walking in the world, but your world will be uplifted naturally and others are invited into this Light-filled space. Very nice!

**Eloise:** To see my purpose as a creator bringing Light is so cool. I guess that was my original purpose. Yes. To bring Light to every form here. Wow. That simple. To make sure the essence of Light remains, or is returned. All I have to do is just show up as Light, which is the most natural thing I have ever done. Okay. I get it.

**Susann:** I'm thrilled for you.

**Eloise:** It is a familiar place. I like it. And I am beginning to glimpse what a natural, effortless impact I can have on people and the situations I am in by holding this Light and carrying its torch like a magic wand of transformation. Yes.

**Susann:** Enjoy. You did great.

**Eloise:** Well, it was good, good work!

# Part Four:

# Tools for Reunion

# 15

# CREATING A SOUL RADIANCE TIMELINE

Take a few minutes at some point to create a Soul radiance timeline for yourself. A timeline punctuates the moments in your life that the brightness of who you are, i.e., your Soul's radiance, came through, even if just as a shooting star across the horizon of your outer world. Your Soul's radiance comes through with your personality and is aligned to a higher truth. There's a knowing, a rightness, felt. There's a sense of connection to something bigger than yourself. You're receptive; the signal is clear; the attunement with Source is alive and well. Do this simply as part of a walking meditation, or through the creation of a ritual space for yourself, or just as a stream-of-consciousness journaling time. Let yourself engage in this creation with a sense of wonder and magic. Let yourself relish the fruits of your Soul's journey. It is a delightful way to recognize that you have been guided by your Soul in more ways than you might imagine at this moment. Your Soul riches are having a way with you whenever your heart is open to allow those riches to be received into your experience. Whenever you choose to let your Soul take you where you long to be, the magic of spirit is ignited in your life.

The first glimpses of our Soul's radiance may show up in simple ways. This might appear as the first time you hopped on a seesaw and felt the freedom of being lifted off the ground and suspended in midair.

Or you might remember a time that you sang your heart out in a school choir, or burst into spontaneous song. I vividly remember the first time I blew a bubble with bubble gum. It was a moment of amazing expansion for me. These moments of self-discovery and coming forward are precious indeed. As you honor these jewels in time, it gives them the opportunity to grow in their value as a part of your life expression.

For example, when I was in college, I found myself contemplating what I wanted to do for a summer job. I flashed on the feeling sensations that poured through me when I was sailing at summer camp years before. Deep inside, I heard an excited, "Yes, that's what I want to do." The next thing I knew I was flying out with my mom to Quanset Sailing Camp for Girls on Cape Cod during spring break so I could interview for the job of sailing instructor. What a grand adventure to get paid for sailing every day on a bay in the ocean with young girls who were keen to learn to sail. To this day, whenever I feel stuck and uncreative about moving into something that is important to me, I reconnect with that wonderful experience of following my heart's passion to sail, and allowing my Soul to take me where I longed to be. The remembrance of this experience frees me to trust where I'm going. My heart and Soul are a tremendous compass for my life's experience.

Allow yourself to take a contemplative view of your life to date, noticing those moments and times when your Soul-Essence revealed itself. Enjoy the revelations and the joy and offer gratitude to your Soul for the ways it has been ever present, holding the torch of your Soul song, burning brightly for you.

# 16

# RECONNECTION
# THROUGH THE HEART

The following tool is effective for reconnecting to all those elements of ourselves that have become disconnected from our Soul, and disconnected from all that is Divine. It works when the disconnection has occurred on the physical and emotional level, especially due to beliefs attached to feelings that have a limiting grip on our sense of self. I find it is best to get in touch with the feeling, not just the mental construct involved, to use this tool as a means for reunion to our Soul's gifts.

For example, do you remember when you fell and skinned your knee when you were a child (or an adult!) and your mom came to you and said, "I'm so sorry"? Then she gave you a hug, and you felt much better. If you still wish you had someone to kiss your boo-boo, so to speak, now is your chance.

The basic principle that worked with that skinned knee for you and your healing applies here. When your mom said, "I'm sorry," she was acknowledging your place of physical pain, but also the place in you where you felt bad about what just happened. Her reaching out transformed the pain in your body and helped you to return to the state of aliveness you felt prior to skinning your knee. When your mom said, "I'm sorry," she was saying, in essence, that she understood: It's okay how you are feeling, and I'm sorry for your moment of falling off your center. She kissed, hugged and gave her love. Your heart and body could then rest and open to love and get reconnected to that wonderful, light-filled little girl or boy, self-stepping into new territory, bicycling on new pavement, running faster than ever before.

So how does this apply to your longing for sacred reunion with all that is Divine and true for you? Here's how. For a moment, put your attention on a physical place of discomfort, or the feeling state you are in that you don't want to stay in. With a feeling, let yourself notice where it is in your body. Feel where it is presenting itself. Put more of your attention on it, for this moment. Really be with it, as though it was a child crying out, "Help me. I don't want it to feel like this." If you have a fear, for instance, and it comes to your attention, realize that it is present to let you know where separation from Soul exists. This is also true of a physical ache or pain. It is letting you know where life force does not flow in your body. It is asking for your attention to remind you of this fact.

Then you simply say, "I'm sorry," and direct those words to the unwanted feeling space within you. You are saying to that emotional aspect within you, or that physical aspect of you, that you are sorry that *you* have allowed disconnection to life and the Divine to occur in the facet of your life that is causing your discomfort. "I'm sorry that I chose coping mechanisms, or anxiety, or anger, or mistrust rather than Soul food to feed this aspect of me. I'm sorry I chose fear over love to guide my life."

Be willing to let your larger sense of self, aware of the discomfort in a part of you, be present and connected, to reunite with that larger connection that you are held in. You do that by saying, "I love you." This opens the heart to allow your Soul, in union with the Divine, to come in and bring life and Divine Love and courage and all that is of the One Spirit. "I love you," allows you to open the door to co-creation with the Divine. Remember, your Soul is connected to all wisdom and knowledge and loving support and universal power to bring exactly what is true for you into the moment, that it may be a moment of reunion with the true source of abundant life. Your Soul knows what is needed. All you have to do is hold the feeling of connection to your Soul-Essence as you say, "I love you," to those less connected parts that are showing themselves in the moment.

Simply by saying, "I'm sorry. I love you," you open the door for your spirit to manifest a reunion with the Divine to that place crying out for reconnection. The old feeling can take a back seat and then dissolve as connection reestablishes itself in the place where the pain showed up.

Simple, quick, potent. And done. Here's a brief summary. Get in touch with the unwanted feeling, emotionally or where it resides in your body. Say, "I'm sorry I have been disconnected here. I love you." (I open to let reconnection happen here). This ignites the process. Repeat it until you feel the magic come in and Light surround the entire situation, inside and out.

Let me give you an example. Not so long ago, I was speaking with one of my relatives, and she spoke to me with a very angry tone. She was displeased with something I had done. I felt an "Ouch!" in my heart area. I outwardly handled the immediate situation calmly, but I was aware that a part of me translated her tone of voice as an attack on my heart.

After the conversation I took a moment to be with my heart. I felt the sensation in my heart and spoke to it. I said, "I'm sorry. I'm so sorry that you are disconnected from the power and the strength you need to support you." No story. No victim. No need to blame or attack back, etc. To the pain in my heart I said, "I'm sorry I am not allowing you to be connected to what you need to feel whole, complete, supported and love-filled. I love you. I now am connecting to our Soul to feed you true food that nourishes and supports you." I added the following phrase I had gained from doing my own journey. "I live in the heart of Love. I rest in the heart of Love." And I breathed this phrase into that area of my heart. I did it a number of times to myself and out loud, making sure I wasn't just mentally repeating the words, but deeply connecting within myself with the beauty of the experience. My heart expanded, relaxed and smiled. It felt strong and easy and happy. It was a delicious reunion with my heart's true resources for life and love.

# 17

# GIVE IT TO GOD PROCESS

There are many spiritual practices that help to awaken the Spirit and remind us that we are spiritual beings. As I spoke of in the chapter entitled "My Soul's Journey," for many of us baby boomers, when we were in our twenties and thirties, awakening our spiritual nature may have meant denouncing some of our physical and emotional capacities. Then came the era of the emotional revolution. We were beating pillows, screaming at the top of our lungs and being radically honest with how we felt. We often did this regardless of those around us. It was vital to get the emotional realm out of the closet for many. It was certainly exciting and enlivening for those of us who had used shutting down as a method of coping during childhood.

Time for the marriage of Spirit and form. How can we bring the beauty of our connection to Spirit into our everyday life? How can we have personal fulfillment without being selfish and full of ego? Must we be meditating or in a synagogue or ashram in order to be spiritual? Isn't it our birthright to be happy, joyful, powerful Souls living abundant lives? Nature, in all its kingdoms, exists and lives fully from that place. Why wouldn't we be designed to know the ecstasy of utter aliveness married with a Soul depth of peaceful union with the Divine?

Well, we are designed that way and anyone can experience it. How to come to that blessed place, you might be asking? I did and others have. We have come to the place of being in love with life itself. And that is what brought the Soul-level work I am doing now into its birthplace. I recognized the need to tap into our Soul resources to replace and displace the emotional wounds we all walk around with. I realized that the one wound is that of separation. Anything we experience in our body, mind or emotional realm that is not ignited by life, is due to some form of separation. I have spent 15 years working from this level. Many wonderful people around the world are also working from this premise. Hallelujah!

Whether it is cancer, MS, lupus, a common cold or a headache. Whether it is sexual abuse, road rage, depression or the feeling of helplessness. Be it mental confusion or a lack of vision or direction. These patterns, and hundreds more, can be resolved with a sense of grand finale when your reconnection, reunion or remembering your connection to the Divine is rekindled where it has been lacking. Your Soul-Essence carries whatever resource is needed.

Your Soul knows and loves to bring you the gift of life wherever it is temporarily lacking. Your Soul loves to reconnect you with the Soul food needed to feed the situation where its lack is pronouncing itself in your body, mind or heart.

I have even found in the last year that a simple process is showing itself, that many are open to, which allows Spirit to fill in, in a moment's notice. The basic premise follows the old saying, "Give it to God."

To try it right now, experience a feeling you would rather not have. Simply feel what is present with you right now. Feel yourself tossing it up to the universe. That can be the hardest part because, more often than not, we get attached to our feelings for various reasons, even though we claim we don't like what we are experiencing. Remember, we created the feeling in ourselves in the first place, so we chose it. Toss the feeling to the universe. Give it to God. Take the emotion you're feeling right now and release it to larger hands and a larger knowledge and perspective.

You are not denouncing it or trying to get rid of it. You are simply asking that Spirit infuse it so that its value be utilized by your Soul in the best way possible. Take a breath and put your attention on a space of universal Light that you wish to create for the feeling to rest in. Create a specific energy stream of Light from that space of universal Light, or "God's Hands," to surround the emotion. Let the Light stream down to the space where you first felt the emotion in your body. For instance, if anger is in the picture, it might be present as a means of moving us out of helplessness. That's an excellent start. If left as anger, it might become ornery or destructive. If you infuse the energy of anger with Spirit, and you hold it as a feeling, not as what you are, it can quickly be transformed to power.

When that energy is brought back into the body, now infused, and held in the place where the anger was, the feeling sensation is known as strength, or confidence, or other hues of power appropriate to the need. This is an example of what it is to merge spirit with form for the purpose of knowing a greater sense of aliveness. This Soul confidence breeds a sense of value and, therefore, a sense of wanting to share and magnify that aliveness, which is the sharing of our Soul gifts and purposes. I certainly don't see any ego or selfish behavior there. Again, anger—a state of emotional reaction—is transformed into power. It is the same energy. Try it on. Power is the same energy as anger, only it is infused with Spirit. I'm not referring to misusing power. That is the state of power over something. Divine power is the true quality of Spirit. Confidence, strength, absoluteness and assurance are some of the manifestations of power in the human expression.

This process of Give it to God, is simple and immediately gratifying. I had a great experience recently of using this process of Give it to God in the following situation. I was feeling a concern about my daughter's financial situation. She is 21 and we are in the process of asking her to step up to the plate and earn more money toward her current living expenses. We had agreed she would work more, and a month later I noticed she hadn't. When my familiar role of mom/caretaker presented itself, fear for her well-being, and anger at her inability to "get it going," were emotions at the top of my list. I had a conversation with her all mapped out in my head, chock-full of how I felt about the situation, and the fact that she should know, and then a light bulb came on. Give it to God. How about remembering that wonderful new way that had come through me to allow Spirit to have a part in the equation? What about letting my Soul guide this moment? So I played with it, and I felt much lighter about it all.

I still carried a bit of righteous motherhood that said I needed to do the responsible thing and at least speak to her about my concerns. Not so emotionally charged—just matter of fact. I then said to myself, "Okay, Soul of mine that is connected to the bounty of All That Is, I will give this one to you and step back and let divine magic lend a loving hand. Then I will open the conversation." The next morning, I spoke to my daughter and in a matter-of-fact way she told me that she was asked to work three more shifts that week at a hostess job that she really enjoys.

Presto. Magic happened. No directive-mothering conversation needed, just many thank-yous to Spirit for showing me how much power it has when I am open to allowing its touch to infuse my life in real and practical ways.

# 18

# GLOBAL RADIANCE

Let's take a moment to discover how our Soul's radiance can have a global impact. If you are reading this book, I suspect you have at least one eye on the planetary picture we are in the midst of creating.

Increasingly there are fabulous avenues opening to participate in making a difference in our world. I would like to contribute the following perspective to give us a Soul-level handle on creating the world we truly wish to be part of.

We manifest the reality we are in divine union with. Imagine what it would be like if everyone was in divine union with a Soul-level DNA and cellular sense of knowing that everything was going to "work out" in alignment with Divine Love and truth. You can substitute your own phrase for this sense of universal, highest good-of-all alignment. Imagine if everyone was aligned with this knowing that all is well, unconquerable life prevails. Then these states would manifest! This state of knowing carries an inherent sense with it that we are all connected, that all is one. Knowing that all is well includes a natural love and compassion for this Earth exactly as it is. Above all, knowing moves beyond faith, it holds no energy of separation or feeling that all is outside our hands and field of influence.

Here's an image to hold. Let's say there are three doors for us, individually and collectively, to choose from. Behind door number one is the sense that all is Divine and I know, for me and my world, "it" is all moving to that Light state of being. Behind door number three is the sense of fear that everything will fail. Look at global warming, all the wars in the world, the lack of clear leadership, etc. It's just a matter of time before "the sky falls." Behind door number two is something in-between. A giant question mark. "I don't know," is the statement it holds. We manifest what we are in divine union with. We manifest what we know in our Soul's core to be true. So, if we hold the knowing that all is well globally, all will be well globally. If our Soul's radiance shines with that knowing, then that will manifest in the collective pattern. If we hold the consciousness of doom and gloom, even though we believe in Spirit's influence and feel we are awakening to the value of Spirit, doom and gloom will happen. Conceptual ideas, even if they are spiritually based, don't manifest. Far too many "spiritual" folks still hold the feeling of being victim to this world's wrongdoings, the doings of others. This still creates door number three—the sky will fall. And door number two manifests by default.

Focus on bringing your Soul riches to life so that you may live as the radiant Soul that you are. Then your joyous fulfillment will connect to the unified world of our collective Soulful creation that manifests global radiance.

# RESOURCES

**To enhance your journey, experience the Guided Meditation
for your Soul-Essence Journey, available on CD at
www.SoulMastery.net**

Susann Taylor Shier presents Soul Mastery and Soul Radiance
workshops, book events, trainings, and teleclasses. She has been
featured on numerous T.V. and radio shows. She travels across
the US and works internationally as a psychotherapist and intuitive
counselor with clients both in person and on the telephone. Her first
book, *Soul Mastery: Accessing the Gifts of Your Soul* was published in
October 2005. She lives in Boulder, Colorado.

To contact Susann for a personal appointment, a Soul-Essence journey, a book presentation, to speak at an event or to conduct a workshop,
e-mail her at susann@soulmastery.net.

Visit www.SoulMastery.net to learn more about the author's work
and for a schedule of her workshops, trainings and teleclasses, and to
purchase her CDs and DVDs.

# REMOVABLE GUIDED MEDITATION FOR YOUR SOUL–ESSENCE JOURNEY

First, put your attention on your breath. Take a few deep breaths to connect with the life force within you that is connected to everything, everywhere. Now bring your awareness to your heart. Breathe into your heart space. Allow yourself to gently consider what it is you wish to experience in this magical journey to your Soul-Essence. Allow your heart to feel a sense of openness around imagining the qualities of Spirit and the quality of experience you wish to connect with as you prepare to be in the field of your Soul-Essence. Take a moment to feel an opening sense of knowing that what you long for is truly possible. Breathe that in.

Now bring your attention back to your breath. Feel, see, sense, get an impression of a universal Light that you know and trust. Feel or see that universal Light. Maybe it's expanded, maybe it's sunlight, maybe it's laser light. Let whatever is true for you of this universal Light in this moment reveal itself. Breathe with it as you honor its abiding presence.

Now sense that Light that you know and trust streaming into your body, beginning with your throat and down to your heart. As you breathe in this presence, take this Light and breath together into your heart space as you allow your heart to open to receive this Light and breath. Feel your heart opening to receive the Light and breath. You are preparing the cells of your body, even your DNA, to receive your Soul-Essence and its gifts and all that it has to bring to you. You are preparing your cells to receive the bounty.

Now allow your whole chest area to expand to take in this Light and breath, bringing that Light and breath now, streaming from your chest area down into your abdomen, opening the cells of your abdomen to take in this breath and Light. Now stream this breath of Light into your pelvic area, down your legs and into your feet, feeling the Light coming all the way through to the soles of your feet. And, bringing that Light back up your legs with your breath, take the Light of this breath into your back and spine, feeling your whole back and spine expanding to receive this universal Light through your breath. As the cells of your back and spine expand to receive this Light, let this Light expand to the back of your neck and into your head. Fill your head with this breath of Light.

Now that your whole body is filled with Light, allow this Light, along with your breath, to expand all around you from the top of your head to the tips of your toes. Feel this Light surrounding you. Maybe it feels like a cloak surrounding you, or it appears like a cloud of Light. Let yourself create this Light as an extension of you. This Light is an extension of you. Feel that Light holding the energy of honor for all that is valuable to you. This Light holds sacred what dwells within your heart and Soul, your very existence and all that you are. Allow yourself to feel the Love and connection of this Light holding sacred all that you are. You are also surrounding yourself with Light to be sure that the only thing that accompanies you to your Soul space is Light.

And now allow this Light that is all around you to move you very easily and gently and naturally beyond this space, time and dimension as you know it into the dimension and the space of your Soul-Essence, as your Soul wishes to bring it to you now. You may feel yourself expanding as Light into a universal dimension beyond yourself that your Soul is connected to, remembering that your Soul and the Light that is around you and the Light with your breath is connected to everything, everywhere. You can now feel yourself expanding to the dimension of your

Soul-Essence. Allow the gifts, the possibilities and all the strengths to come to you from your Soul in this moment in time, to come to you for you to merge with.

Trust that your Soul longs to take you where you wish to be. It will bring to you a gift of *you*, the resource of *you* that you are wishing to reunite with at this time. Open yourself to receive it. You may also wish to connect with your Soul-Essence through the sensation of moving down a passageway, a passageway of your own creation, knowing that at the end of this passageway, that you move through in your own pace and time, there will be an opening. That opening may be wide, it may be a door, it doesn't matter; just know that there will be an opening there. And, as you move through that opening, you will be touching into the space of your Soul-Essence.

Let yourself walk freely and openly into that space, knowing you are surrounded by the Light that holds sacred all that you wish to merge with and reunite with. And then feel yourself as an explorer, allowing this journey to bring you into a magical dimension, the exploration of your Soul-Essence. Seeing, feeling, touching, sensing what is there. Being with it, creating with it. Whatever shows up, trust it to be true to you and your Soul. Allow it its space within you. Just be with what comes to you, allow yourself to just move through this field of your Soul-Essence as you commune with it. Notice what's there.

Enjoy, explore. You may ask for greater wisdom and knowledge. You may ask for greater depth and understanding. You may ask for greater Love and connection. And see what presents itself to you as you do so. Take your time. Be in this space as long as you wish. Allow the sounds to carry you into the depth of what your Soul wishes to bring to you. And, when you feel you have received what it is that is valuable to you, the treasures, the gifts, the strengths, and the purposes for this journey, you can move at your pace to the next section below.

# After the Completion of Your Journey to Your Soul-Essence

There you are, in union with your Soul and its gifts and its resources in new ways that are real and true to what matters to you at this time in your life. Begin to put your attention again on breathing Light into your body. Then begin to breathe these resources that you have just reunited with into your body. You are breathing these resources into your body so that they can become even more real in your life, as a continual extension of you. Feel yourself taking in what it is that you've just experienced. Maybe it's an expanse, a color, a Light, a whole story, an image or many symbols. Surround with Light the dimension you've just created from the reunion with your Soul-Essence.

Feel this dimension of your Soul-Essence you have created surrounded with Light and stream it now into your heart. Allow your heart to receive this gift. Feel your heart expanding, and if it was just a color, or energy, or a sensation that you experienced, give it a picture. Maybe there's an image or color that you saw, or a sound you heard, or a sensation you had that can create a picture to bring into your heart so your heart can hold a specific place for this symbol for you. Feel your heart receiving that symbol that is the gift of your Soul. It is now present within you to be a real part of you. This will be useful so that anytime you wish to connect with the All That Is that your Soul-Essence is bringing to you, you can just imagine that symbol in your heart. And your whole body will smile for the connection and the gift.

Now take that symbol, that experience, that sensation, that impression, and stream it, surrounded by Light, down into your abdomen. This space of your abdomen I call the womb space of creation, your creation, the space from which you create. As you bring this space alive with this dimension of your Soul gift, feel what it feels like to hold that within you. Feel the knowing you are having now of how real it is to carry this dimension of yourself within you, and feel what it feels like to manifest from this space, to create from this quality of Spirit that you are, that you embody. Take your time as you breathe in this greater aspect of your Soul.

You are now one with it. It abides with you. It lives as you. You might wish to make a declaration at this point along these lines: I am this, this abides within me, and I create from within this space. Feel the power of the declaration. And, then, if you wish, again at your own time and pace, feel what it's like to walk in the world from this space. You can take a moment to imagine different scenarios in your life and what it feels like to walk into those scenarios, as aspects of your Soul-Essence, from this place you just created. Again declaring, "I walk in the world as this new creation. I am this, and this world is blessed because of my presence in this way." Allow yourself to be Soulfully radiant. This is your Soul's radiance coming forward as you allow yourself to radiate from all that you are, holding the joy, the power, the connection and the grace of union with all that you hold sacred of your Soul.

As you complete this portion of your journey to your Soul-Essence, take a moment to offer appreciation to your Soul and the universal connection that is always held for you. Offer appreciation to your Soul for all it has eternally been connected to for you, opening the field of all knowledge, all possibilities, all Love and connection for you to experience in abundance.

CPSIA information can be obtained at www.ICGtesting.com
Printed in the USA
BVOW09s1853120214

344718BV00002B/431/P